RON ROBISON

The Wobble Factor

Reclaiming Faith for Your Journey

Copyright © 2026 by Ron Robison

All rights reserved. No part of this publication may be reproduced, stored, or transmitted in any form or by any means, electronic, mechanical, photocopying, recording, scanning, or otherwise without written permission from the publisher. It is illegal to copy this book, post it to a website, or distribute it by any other means without permission.

First edition

This book was professionally typeset on Reedsy. Find out more at reedsy.com

Contents

Introduction — 1

I The Myth We've Been Sold

1. The Straight Line Deception — 7
2. The Gap Between Pew and Practice — 12

II The Reality of the Wobble

3. What Is the Wobble Factor? — 21
4. The Wobble as Navigation — 31
5. Recognizing Your Pattern — 42

III The Framework for Forward Momentum

6. The Pilocon Principles — 57
7. Tools for the Journey — 69
8. Community in the Wobble — 82

IV Living the Wobble

9. Embracing the Tension — 97
10. The Long View — 111

11. Conclusion — 124

About the Author — 133

Introduction

The Myth We've Been Sold

We've been taught that mature faith is a steady, linear climb—a march directly toward the Cross with seamless growth and unwavering stability. But for every disciple who has honestly assessed their own journey, this "straight line" model is a profound myth that leads only to shame and self-condemnation when we inevitably stumble.

The Reality of Christian Discipleship

The Wobble Factor reveals what every honest Christian knows but rarely admits: discipleship is not a march—it's a wobble. The reality of Christian growth is constant, necessary course-correction inherent in a life guided by the Holy Spirit. It's the perpetual tension between conviction and compromise, certainty and doubt, zeal and wisdom.

Every mistake, every correction, every moment of drift and recovery is part of the process. The wobble is not a sign of failure; it's the signature of growth—proof that you are engaged in the dynamic, difficult work of maturing in Christ.

What You'll Discover

This foundational book dismantles the performance trap that keeps Christians hiding their struggles and provides a framework for authentic discipleship:

- Why the straight line is a deception that creates shame, comparison, and

spiritual exhaustion
- How to recognize your personal wobble pattern and distinguish productive navigation from destructive drift
- The Pilocon Principles: six core principles built on personal responsibility that guide faithful navigation
- Practical tools for the journey including Scripture engagement, prayer practices, authentic community, and self-assessment
- How to embrace tension without collapsing it—holding conviction and compromise, certainty and doubt, zeal and wisdom
- The long view: measuring progress over decades and finding freedom in accepting you'll never "arrive"

Built on a Foundation of Personal Responsibility

Drawing on the author's decades of experience as an Air Force weather forecaster, athlete, pastor, and disciple, _The Wobble Factor_ uses the powerful metaphor of harbor pilot navigation to illustrate how discipleship actually works. Just as a harbor pilot makes hundreds of micro-adjustments to safely guide a ship to dock, disciples navigate through constantly changing conditions—not in a straight line, but through faithful course correction.

At the core is a simple but revolutionary truth: You control exactly two things in your discipleship—your actions and your attitudes. Everything else flows from taking full responsibility for these.

Who This Book Is For

- Christians exhausted from performing spiritual maturity they don't feel
- Believers struggling with the gap between their Sunday persona and Monday reality
- Disciples who wonder if they're failing because they're still struggling with issues they thought they'd overcome
- Anyone tired of comparing their messy journey to others' highlight reels
- Church leaders wanting to create cultures of authenticity rather than

performance

The Invitation

The Wobble Factor isn't here to erase your wobble, but to help you recognize its pattern, embrace the process, and learn how to steer toward truth when the waters get rough. This is an invitation to stop performing discipleship and start practicing it—to navigate faithfully through whatever conditions you encounter, one honest, responsible step at a time.

Because the wobble isn't a bug in your discipleship. It's how discipleship actually works.

I

The Myth We've Been Sold

1

The Straight Line Deception

The testimony format is a lie. Not the testimonies themselves—those are often genuine accounts of God's work in people's lives. But the *format* is a lie. The structure we've been handed for sharing our faith stories creates an impossibly tidy narrative: I was lost, then I was found, and now I'm steadily climbing toward spiritual maturity.

It's a three-act play with a clean resolution. Act One - my life before Christ (usually terrible). Act Two - my conversion moment (usually dramatic). Act Three - my transformed life (usually triumphant). Roll credits. The problem is that Act Three never actually ends. And it's rarely triumphant.

What we don't share - what gets edited out of the Sunday morning spotlight - is the mess that comes after the conversion. The confusion. The backsliding. The days when you wonder if any of it was real. The moments when you choose poorly despite knowing better. The patterns you thought were broken that suddenly reassert themselves with surprising strength.

We've been sold a straight line when the reality is far more complex.

The Idealized Trajectory

Open any book on spiritual formation and you'll find some version of the diagram of a line moving steadily upward and to the right. The x-axis represents time; the y-axis represents spiritual maturity, closeness to God, or Christ-likeness. The message is clear, if you're doing this right, you should see consistent, measurable progress.

Church culture reinforces this narrative at every turn. We celebrate the "radical transformation" stories. We create programs with clearly defined stages:

1. Seeker
2. New believer
3. Growing Christian
4. Mature disciple
5. Leader

We teach that sanctification is a process, yes, but we imply it's a *predictable* process - one that moves in a single direction if you follow the right steps. The language we use betrays our assumptions:

- "Growing in faith" (always upward)
- "Moving forward" (always ahead)
- "Falling away" (the only recognized regression)
- "Backsliding" (a failure state, not a normal occurrence)

This idealized trajectory becomes the measuring stick against which we assess ourselves and others. Are you further along than you were last year? Are you more spiritually mature than that person? Have you graduated from "baby Christian" to "solid believer"? The straight line becomes both our aspiration and our accusation.

Where This Myth Comes From

The straight line deception didn't emerge from thin air. It has sources, and understanding them helps us see why the myth has such power over us.

The Testimony Template: Since the early church, conversion stories have been central to Christian witness. But somewhere along the way, we standardized them. Paul's Damascus Road experience became the model, a dramatic before and after, with the "after" portrayed as unambiguously better. This works beautifully for evangelism. It's less helpful for discipleship.

The Self-Help Industrial Complex: The church has absorbed more from secular personal development culture than we'd like to admit. The promise of continuous improvement, the emphasis on measurable outcomes, and the belief that the right technique or system will produce reliable results. These are all borrowed frameworks that don't translate well to spiritual formation.

Our Discomfort with Paradox: Western Christianity, in particular, struggles with holding tension. We want clarity, certainty, and resolution. The idea that spiritual growth might include regression, that maturity might look like increasing awareness of our brokenness, and that faithfulness might sometimes feel like failure are paradoxes that make us deeply uncomfortable. So we flatten them into a simple upward trajectory.

The Platform Effect: We hear only certain kinds of stories from the stage of the church. The person who has "overcome" gets the microphone. The person still struggling stays in their seat. This creates a survivorship bias in our collective narrative. We only see the success stories, so we assume success is the norm and our struggles are the exception.

The Hidden Cost

The straight line myth doesn't just fail to describe reality, it actively harms us.

Shame: When your experience doesn't match the expected trajectory, you assume something is wrong with *you*. You're not praying enough, not reading Scripture enough, not surrendering enough. The problem must be your lack of effort or faith. The myth transforms every wobble into a personal failure.

Comparison: If discipleship is a linear climb, then it's easy to look around and assess who's "ahead" and who's "behind." We become judges of spiritual progress in both others and ourselves. This breeds either pride "I'm further along than them" or despair "everyone else seems to have this figured out".

Performance: When you believe you should be consistently moving forward, you learn to perform or fake progress. You say the right things in small group. You volunteer for the right ministries. You cultivate the appearance of spiritual maturity because the alternative of admitting you're stuck, confused, or regressing feels like admitting failure.

Spiritual Exhaustion: The pressure to maintain the illusion of steady progress is relentless. You can't afford to have a bad week, a season of doubt, or a pattern you thought was resolved suddenly resurface. The straight line demands constant vigilance and improvement. It's exhausting.

Isolation: Perhaps most damaging, the myth isolates us from one another. If everyone is pretending to move steadily forward, no one can admit they're struggling. We sit in church services surrounded by people, all of us hiding our reality, all of us assuming we're the only one who doesn't have it together.

The straight line myth creates a church full of actors performing a play about discipleship rather than actual disciples stumbling toward Jesus.

The Honest Assessment

Here's what every honest disciple knows but rarely says out loud:

- Some weeks you feel close to God. Other weeks you don't.
- Some seasons you're eager to pray and read Scripture. Other seasons it feels like drudgery.
- Some years you grow significantly. Other years you seem to be treading water or even moving backward.

You have the same argument with your spouse that you had five years ago. You fall into the same sin pattern you thought you'd conquered. You doubt things you were certain about. You become certain about things you used to doubt. You have moments of profound clarity followed by months of fog. You experience breakthrough followed by breakdown. You take three steps forward and two steps back, or sometimes two steps forward and three steps back.

> *This isn't failure. This is reality.*

The problem isn't your experience—the problem is the myth that tells you your experience is abnormal.

> What if the wobble isn't a bug in the system? What if it's a feature?
>
> What if the course corrections, the mistakes, the drift and recovery—what if all of that is exactly how discipleship works?

> *That's the question we're going to explore. But first, we need to look more closely at the gap between what we present on Sunday morning and what we experience on Monday.*

2

The Gap Between Pew and Practice

It's Sunday morning and you know exactly who you're supposed to be. You walk into the sanctuary with your Bible, your coffee, maybe a donut and your practiced smile. You greet people warmly. You sing the songs with your hands raised (or not, depending on your tradition and comfort level). You nod knowingly during the sermon, maybe even give an "Amen". You discuss the main points in your Sunday School class or small group with thoughtful insights and relevant Scripture references.

You know your lines. You play your part.

It's Monday morning and you're not sure who you are. The alarm goes off and you ignore it. You snap at your kids over breakfast. You zone out in the meeting. You gossip about a coworker. You look at things online you shouldn't. You choose comfort over obedience, convenience over conviction, your will over God's. You forget your lines. You drop the mask.

The distance between these two versions of yourself - the Sunday version and the Monday version - is what I call the gap. And if we're honest, it's not just a gap between two days of the week. It's the gap between the disciple you present yourself to be and the person you actually are.

Sunday Morning vs. Monday Reality

The church service is a carefully curated experience. Everything is polished, timed, and designed to create a specific atmosphere. The music builds to an emotional crescendo. The sermon offers clear principles and actionable steps. The testimonies showcase transformation. Even the lighting is optimized to create the right mood.

There's nothing inherently wrong with any of this. Worship gatherings should be intentional and well-executed. But the unintended consequence is that we create a space where everything looks *resolved*. People appear joyful, faithful, and together. Problems are presented as past tense, "I *was* struggling with anger, but God has been working in my life."

Then Monday arrives. The bills are still due. The marriage is still strained. The addiction still whispers. The anxiety still tightens your chest. The same patterns reassert themselves. The same struggles resurface. The Monday version of your life doesn't feel like the triumphant "after" photo from Sunday's testimony. It feels messy, complicated, and unresolved. You're not sure how to connect Sunday's inspiration with Monday's reality.

This gap creates cognitive dissonance. It leaves you to wonder, "Is everyone else actually living the victorious Christian life while I'm faking it?" Or is everyone else faking it too? The answer, of course, is that almost everyone is experiencing some version of the gap. But because no one talks about it openly, we each assume we're the exception.

The Performance Trap

The gap wouldn't be so problematic if we simply acknowledged it. If we could say, "Sunday is the ideal we're aiming for, and Monday is the messy process of getting there," we'd be fine. The problem is that we've learned to *perform* discipleship rather than *practice* it.

Performance discipleship looks like this. You memorize the right answers for small group discussion questions, even if you don't actually live them out. You volunteer for visible ministry roles to demonstrate commitment.

You post Bible verses on social media to signal your faith. You use Christian language fluently as you talk about "surrendering to God's will" and "walking in obedience" while your actual daily decisions tell a different story. You become skilled at looking like a disciple without doing the difficult work of becoming one.

This isn't necessarily conscious deception. Most of us aren't deliberately trying to fool anyone. We're responding to the incentive structure we've been placed in. Church culture rewards the appearance of spiritual maturity. It celebrates the "got it together" Christian. It gives platform and authority to those who can articulate the faith convincingly.

What it doesn't reward—and often subtly punishes—is honest struggle.

Try this experiment. Next Sunday, when someone asks how you're doing, respond with complete honesty such as, "I'm actually really struggling with doubt right now. I'm not sure I believe half of what we're singing about." Or, "My prayer life is non-existent. I haven't opened my Bible in weeks, and I'm not even sure I care." Watch what happens. At best, you'll get an awkward pause followed by a promise to pray for you. At worst, you'll be seen as spiritually weak, in need of intervention, or possibly backsliding. The message is clear, don't bring your Monday reality to Sunday morning.

So we don't. We perform instead.

Why We Hide Our Struggles

The reasons for hiding are layered and complex, but they generally fall into a few categories:

Shame: We're embarrassed that we're not further along. We've been Christians for five, ten, twenty years so shouldn't we have this figured out by now? Admitting we're still struggling with basic issues feels like admitting failure.

Fear of Judgment: We've seen how the church community responds to obvious sin or public failure. We know there's a category for "backslider" or "struggling believer," and we don't want to be placed in it. Better to keep up appearances than risk being marginalized.

Protecting Others: Sometimes we hide because we don't want to be a stumbling block. If we admit our doubts, might we cause someone else to doubt? If we acknowledge our ongoing sin patterns, might we give others permission to stay in theirs? So we stay quiet for the sake of others.

Protecting the Gospel: We've been taught that our lives are a testimony to others. If we reveal our messiness, won't that undermine our witness? Won't non-believers point to our hypocrisy and reject the faith? So we maintain our performance for the sake of the Gospel.

Exhaustion: Sometimes we hide simply because we're tired of trying to explain. Tired of the well-meaning advice. Tired of being told to pray more, trust more, surrender more. It's easier to say "I'm fine" than to wade into the complexity of what's actually happening.

> All of these reasons are understandable. None of them lead to genuine transformation.

What This Costs Us

The gap between performance and reality extracts a steep price:

Stunted Growth: You can't grow past problems you won't acknowledge. When you're busy maintaining the appearance of spiritual maturity, you're not actually doing the work of maturing. The performance becomes a substitute for the process.

Fractured Identity: Living with a significant gap between your public and private self creates internal fragmentation. You're not one person - you're two, the Sunday version and the Monday version. Over time, you're not even sure which one is really you.

Missed Connection: The deepest, most transformative relationships happen when people meet each other in their actual reality, not their performed version. By hiding behind the mask, you rob yourself and others of genuine connection. You remain surrounded by people but fundamentally alone.

Wasted Energy: Maintaining a performance is exhausting. The energy you spend managing your image, crafting your responses, and hiding your struggles is energy that could be directed toward actual growth and healing.

False Assurance: Perhaps most dangerous, the performance can fool even you. You can start to believe your own act. You confuse your ability to talk about faith with actually having faith. You mistake your knowledge of spiritual disciplines for actually practicing them. The gap becomes invisible because you've convinced yourself the Sunday version is the real you.

The Question We're Afraid to Ask

If we're honest, there's a question lurking beneath all of this, a question we're afraid to voice because it feels like it undermines everything:

> If discipleship requires this much performance, this much pretending, this much gap between what we claim and what we experience…
> is any of it real?

That's the question that haunts us in the 3 AM darkness. That's the doubt we push down when we're singing with hands raised on Sunday morning. That's the fear that keeps us locked in the performance. Because if we stop performing—if we let people see the Monday reality—we're terrified we'll discover there's nothing underneath. That we've been faking it for so long, we've forgotten what genuine faith even feels like.

But here's what I want you to consider: Maybe the performance itself is what's preventing you from discovering what's real. Maybe the gap exists not because you're failing at discipleship, but because you're trying to practice a version of discipleship that doesn't actually exist.

Maybe the wobble, the drift and correction, the struggle and recovery, the gap between intention and action isn't something to hide. Maybe it's the territory where real transformation happens.

Maybe it's time to stop performing the straight line and start navigating the wobble.

II

The Reality of the Wobble

3

What Is the Wobble Factor?

A harbor pilot is a specialist navigator who boards incoming ships to guide them safely through treacherous coastal waters into port. These are some of the most skilled mariners in the world, with intimate knowledge of their specific harbor, every sandbar, every current, every quirk of the tide.

Something remarkable is that even with all that expertise, a harbor pilot never steers a ship in a perfectly straight line. Watch a ship approach harbor and you'll see constant, subtle course corrections. A degree or two to port. A slight adjustment to starboard. The pilot is perpetually responding to wind, current, the ship's momentum, traffic patterns, and a dozen other variables that are never exactly the same twice.

> *The ship reaches the dock not because it traveled in a straight line, but because the pilot made hundreds of micro-adjustments along the way. That's the wobble. And that's actual, authentic discipleship.*

Defining the Wobble

The Wobble Factor is the constant, necessary course correction inherent in a life guided by the Holy Spirit. It's not the absence of direction, rather it's the presence of dynamic navigation. Your desired destination is to become more Christ-like, and in closer union with the Father. But the journey toward that destination is never linear because you're not traveling through static conditions. You're navigating through:

- Changing circumstances (job loss, health crisis, relational upheaval)
- Internal weather (doubt, depression, spiritual dryness, unexpected joy)
- Cultural currents (shifting values, new challenges, evolving understanding)
- Relational dynamics (community influence, accountability, isolation)
- Your own evolving maturity (what you couldn't see before becomes visible; what seemed certain becomes questionable)

> *The wobble is what happens when you try to maintain course to Christ-likeness through all of those conditions.*

One week you're gripped by conviction about simplifying your life. You're ready to sell everything and live radically for Jesus. The next week you're paying bills and the radical conviction feels naive. That's the wobble between zeal and wisdom.

You read a passage of Scripture that transforms your understanding of God's character. You're filled with certainty. Then you encounter suffering, yours or someone else's, that seems incompatible with that understanding. Now you're wrestling with doubt. That's the wobble between certainty and doubt.

You commit to a spiritual discipline such as daily prayer, regular fasting, consistent Scripture reading. You do well for three weeks, then life gets chaotic and the discipline falls apart. You feel like you've failed, but then you restart with adjusted expectations. That's the wobble between conviction and compromise.

> The wobble is not a sign of failure. It's the signature of growth. It's proof that you're engaged in the dynamic, difficult work of maturing in Christ rather than performing a static role without growth.

Three Core Tensions

The wobble manifests most clearly in three perpetual tensions that every disciple navigates:

1) Conviction and Compromise

You know what you believe. You have convictions about how you should live, what you should prioritize, how you should steward your resources and relationships. These convictions come from Scripture, from the Holy Spirit's leading, from your understanding of what it means to follow Jesus.

But you also live in the world. You have responsibilities, limitations, relationships with people who don't share your convictions. You have a body that gets tired, a mind that gets overwhelmed, circumstances that are genuinely complex. The wobble happens in the space between.

You're convicted that you should be more generous, but you're also trying to save for retirement. You believe in radical hospitality, but you also need boundaries to protect your family's wellbeing. You want to stand firm on biblical truth, but you also want to love your neighbor who sees things differently.

This isn't hypocrisy—it's navigation. You're trying to faithfully and authentically live out your convictions in a world that rarely offers clean, simple choices. Sometimes you lean too far toward uncompromising conviction and become rigid, judgmental, or disconnected from reality. Other times you lean too far toward accommodation and lose your distinctiveness, your saltiness, your prophetic edge.

The wobble is the constant recalibration between these conviction and promise.

2) Certainty and Doubt

You want to be certain about God's existence, His character, His promises, His will for your life. Certainty feels like faith. Doubt feels like its opposite. But then you encounter mystery, unanswered prayer, suffering that doesn't make sense, Biblical passages that seem contradictory, and theological questions without tidy answers. People you respect may believe different things with equal conviction.

Or maybe your doubt is more visceral than intellectual. You wake up one day and the faith that felt solid yesterday feels hollow today. You pray and sense nothing. You read Scripture and it's just words on a page. You look at your life and can't clearly see God's hand anywhere. The wobble happens when you try to remain faithful in the midst of doubt.

It's the tension between "Lord, I believe" and "Help my unbelief"—often in the same breath, sometimes in the same sentence. It's continuing to follow Jesus even when you're not entirely sure He's there. It's holding your theology with conviction while acknowledging the limits of your understanding.

Some seasons you're pulled more toward certainty—you see God's faithfulness clearly, Scripture comes alive, prayer feels vital and real. Other seasons you're pulled more toward doubt—everything that felt certain becomes questionable, nothing seems clear.

> *The wobble is remaining engaged in the journey even when your confidence in the map fluctuates.*

3) Zeal and Wisdom

When you first encounter a truth, when the Holy Spirit awakens something in you, when you see clearly what God is calling you to you feel zeal. Passionate, uncompromising, ready-to-act-immediate zeal. Zeal is beautiful! It's the fuel that launches movements, plants churches, drives mission work, sparks reformation. Without zeal, faith becomes mere intellectual assent, a cultural inheritance rather than a lived reality. But zeal without wisdom is dangerous. Unchecked zeal burns out. It makes promises it can't keep. It judges others harshly for not matching its intensity. It mistakes its own passion for God's leading. It can be manipulated, misdirected, or weaponized. Wisdom tempers zeal. It asks:

- Is this sustainable?

- Is this timing right?
- Have I considered the full implications?
- Am I accounting for my own limitations and blind spots?
- What are the long term effects of this decision?

But wisdom without zeal is equally dangerous. Wisdom can become an excuse for inaction. It can rationalize away costly obedience. It can analyze and discuss and consider until the moment for action has passed. It can become so measured and careful that it loses the ability to take risks or respond to the Spirit's prompting.

> The wobble is the constant negotiation between these two.

You feel called to something radical—and you need to discern whether that's the Holy Spirit or your own ego. You're urged toward caution—and you need to discern whether that's wisdom or fear. You want to act boldly—but you also want to act wisely. Sometimes those align perfectly. Often they create tension.

> *The wobble is learning when to step on the gas and when to pump the brakes, when to trust your zeal and when to consult wisdom, when to move quickly and when to wait.*

Biblical Examples of the Wobble

If you're still not convinced that the wobble is normal, that it's actually how discipleship works, let's look at some of the patterns in Scripture.

Peter's Wobble: Peter is perhaps the most vivid example of wobble in the New Testament. This is a man who:

- Declares Jesus is the Messiah, the Son of the living God (certainty).
- Immediately tries to rebuke Jesus for talking about crucifixion and gets

called "Satan" for it (misguided zeal).
- Promises he'll never deny Jesus (conviction).
- Denies Jesus three times before the rooster crows (compromise under pressure)
- Preaches boldly at Pentecost (zeal).
- Later withdraws from eating with Gentiles when certain Jews arrive, earning public correction from Paul (compromise).

Peter wasn't a failure. He became a pillar of the early church. But his journey wasn't a straight line—it was a wobble. Each mistake, each course correction, each moment of weakness followed by recovery was part of his formation.

Paul's Wobble: Paul, the great apostle, the author of much of the New Testament, also wobbled:

- He's absolutely certain of the gospel, defending it fiercely against any compromise (conviction).
- He becomes "all things to all people," adapting his approach based on his audience (wisdom-informed flexibility).
- He wrestles with his "thorn in the flesh," pleading with God to remove it (doubt about God's plan).
- He learns to accept that God's grace is sufficient in his acceptance of the thorn (certainty in God's purpose).
- He experiences profound spiritual revelations (certainty).
- He admits he doesn't fully understand but presses on anyway (navigating mystery).

Even Paul - probably the most influential Christian leader following Jesus' death - was constantly navigating tensions, making adjustments, and learning through experience.

David's Wobble: David is called "a man after God's own heart," but his story is one extended wobble:

- Deep devotion to God alternating with massive moral failures.
- Profound trust in God's promises alongside seasons of fear and hiding.
- Worship and warfare, poetry and violence, faith and cunning.
- Genuine repentance followed by problematic patterns reasserting themselves in his life.

The Psalms themselves capture the wobble perfectly. Sometimes in a single psalm you'll see David swing from despair to confidence, from complaint to praise, from feeling abandoned to trusting God's presence.

The Disciples' Collective Wobble: The twelve disciples as a group demonstrate the wobble throughout the Gospels:

- They leave everything to follow Jesus (zeal).
- They consistently misunderstand His mission (needing correction).
- They're given authority and see miracles (certainty).
- They fail to cast out a demon and Jesus questions their faith (doubt).
- They promise to stay with Jesus no matter what (conviction).
- They all flee when He's arrested (compromise under pressure).
- They see the resurrected Christ and worship (certainty).
- Some still doubt after the resurrection (ongoing wobble).

> Even after Pentecost, the early church wobbles. The Jerusalem Council debates how to handle Gentile believers. Paul and Barnabas have a sharp disagreement and part ways. Churches struggle with division, false teaching, and navigating their relationship to the surrounding culture.

Why We've Missed This Pattern

If the wobble is so clearly the pattern of discipleship throughout Scripture, why have we missed it? Why have we believed in the straight line instead?

We read backward: When we encounter Peter in Acts, we know how his story turns out. We know he becomes a pillar of the church, so we read his earlier failures as "just a phase" he grew past. We flatten his three-dimensional journey into a simple before-and-after narrative.

We emphasize resolution: When we teach these stories, we focus on the moments of triumph - Peter's confession, Paul's conversion, David's victory over Goliath. We minimize or skim past the wobble moments because they're less inspiring and harder to package into a clean teaching point.

We moralize the failures: We turn the wobble moments into cautionary tales, "Don't be like Peter and deny Jesus," "Don't be like David and commit adultery", rather than recognizing them as normal parts of the discipleship process. *This turns biblical characters into moral examples (good or bad) rather than fellow travelers showing us their journey.*

We forget they didn't know the ending: When David is hiding in caves from Saul, he doesn't know he'll become king. When Peter denies Jesus, he doesn't know about the resurrection three days away. They were navigating in real time, without the benefit of knowing how their story ends. Just like us.

The Wobble Is Not...

Before we go further, let's clarify what the wobble is not:

The wobble is not an excuse for sin. Recognizing that course correction is normal doesn't mean we shrug off destructive patterns or deliberate disobedience. The wobble is about navigating complex tensions, not about justifying behavior we know is sin.

The wobble is not the same as drifting. Drifting is passive as you're carried by currents without awareness or intention. A wobble is a point of active navigation where a disciple is intentionally engaged, aware, and making corrections. We'll explore this distinction more in the next chapter.

The wobble is not perpetual chaos. While the journey isn't linear, it does have direction. Over time, over years, you should see overall movement toward Christ-likeness, even if the path zigzags. If you're just spinning in circles with no net forward movement, that's not wobble - it's something else that needs special attention.

The wobble is not a reason to abandon conviction. You still need fixed points or truths you hold firm, convictions you won't compromise. Acknowledging the wobble affects how you live those out in complex situations, not in whether they're true.

The Signature of Growth

Here's the reframe of your thinking that I want to offer: ***The wobble isn't evidence that something's wrong with your discipleship. It's evidence that discipleship is actually happening.***

Growth requires adjustment. Learning requires mistakes. Formation requires tension. Navigation requires course correction. If your faith looks exactly the same as it did five years ago with the same certainties, same practices, same understanding, no tensions or questions, that's not stability. That's stagnation.

The wobble means you're alive. You're engaged. You're responding to the Spirit's leading even when it takes you into uncomfortable territory. You're grappling with real questions instead of settling for easy answers. You're being shaped rather than staying static. The wobble is the signature of growth with active proof that you're becoming, not just being. Proof that you're following a living God who's leading you somewhere, not maintaining a dead religion that keeps you in place.

So the question isn't: "How do I eliminate the wobble?"

The question is: "How do I navigate it well?"

That's what we're going to explore next.

4

The Wobble as Navigation

There's a critical distinction we need to make, and your spiritual health might depend on understanding it:

> *Not all movement is navigation.*

You can be in constant, exhausting motion and still be drifting. You can feel the wind and waves, experience the pull of currents, and mistake all that activity for progress. But if you're not actively steering, if you have no reference points, if you're simply being carried by forces you're not engaging with, you're not navigating, you're just moving. The difference between wobble and drift is the difference between navigating the sea and being lost at sea.

What Is Navigation?

Navigation is the art and science of determining your position then charting a course to a known destination. It requires three essential elements:

First, you need to know where you are. Not where you wish you were, not where you're supposed to be, not where you were last week. Where you actually are, right now, in your current condition with your current limitations and your current resources.

Second, you need to know where you're going. You need a destination, a heading, a direction of travel. You don't necessarily need to see the entire route mapped out, but you need to know what you're aiming for.

Third, you need fixed points for reference. In maritime navigation, these fixed points are landmarks, celestial bodies, or GPS coordinates. These are things that don't move with you, that remain constant so you can measure your position relative to them.

Without these three elements, you're not navigating. You're just hoping.

The Harbor Pilot Metaphor

Let's return to the harbor pilot image, because it's central to understanding how the wobble works. When a harbor pilot boards a ship, he or she doesn't immediately know everything about how that particular vessel will handle. Every ship is unique with a different size, different weight distribution, different engine response, and different turning radius. The pilot has to feel how each specific ship responds.

The harbor pilot doesn't know the exact conditions he or she will encounter on any specific transit. The tide tables provide general information, but the actual current strength varies. The weather forecast predicts wind, but the actual gusts are unpredictable. There might be traffic that wasn't there an hour ago.

So the pilot navigates by constant feedback and adjustments by making a course change s and observing how the ship responds. Too sluggish? Adjust earlier next time. Too sharp? Use less rudder. The pilot feels the current pushing the ship and has to compensate or sees traffic ahead and has to modify the ship's course. Then the tide has shifts and has to recalculate the approach angle to the dock.

This is active, engaged, responsive navigation. It looks like wobble from the outside with all of the course corrections and the meandering line on the chart, but it's not random movement. Every adjustment serves the goal of safely reaching the dock.

That's also what spiritual navigation looks like.

The Wobble: Navigation with Purpose

The wobble is what happens when you're *actively engaged* in steering your life toward Christ while responding to real conditions. What about the reality in practice?

Navigating Conviction and Compromise: You're convicted about simplicity and generosity. You want to live with open hands, trusting God's provision rather than accumulating security. That's your heading—your direction of travel. But you also have actual responsibilities. Children to feed. A spouse with different risk tolerance. Aging parents who might need care. A job market that requires certain credentials and positioning. The wobble happens as you navigate between the conviction and the reality.

You make a decision to downsize your home—moving toward simplicity. But you discover you actually need more space than you thought for your family to function well so you adjust. You increase your giving significantly leaning into generosity. But you also maintain an emergency fund because total financial precariousness would create anxiety that hinders your spiritual life, so you adjust. An adjustment isn't abandoning the conviction. It's steering toward it through actual conditions. You're navigating.

Navigating Certainty and Doubt: You believe God is good, sovereign, and present. That's your fixed point or the North Star you're navigating by. But then your child gets sick. Really sick. You pray with all the faith you can muster. Nothing changes. Months pass. You watch your child suffer and you start to wonder: Is God actually good? Is He listening? Is He even there? The wobble happens as you navigate this tension.

Some days you lean hard into certainty as you pray, you claim promises, you trust. Other days doubt crashes over you and you can barely get through your prayers. You keep showing up to church even when it feels hollow because you know the doubt might be temporary. You're honest with safe people about your struggle. You give yourself permission to question while maintaining connection to the community of faith. You haven't abandoned your belief, you're navigating through conditions that make belief difficult. You're staying engaged even in the fog.

Navigating Zeal and Wisdom: You encounter a new understanding of what it means to follow Jesus, maybe through a book, a sermon, a conversation, or a personal revelation. You're gripped by it. You want to reorganize your entire life around this truth immediately. That's zeal and it's good.

But wisdom asks questions like the following. Is this sustainable? Have you tested this against Scripture and counsel? Are you accounting for your responsibilities? Is the timing right? The wobble happens as you navigate between the urgent pull of zeal and the measured counsel of wisdom.

You take a step in the direction your zeal is pulling you—maybe you commit to a new discipline, redirect some resources, or have a difficult conversation. But you also build in accountability, set a timeline to evaluate, and give yourself permission to adjust based on what you learn. You move forward but not recklessly. You stay open to course correction but don't let caution paralyze you. You're navigating. Each adjustment serves your forward movement rather than undermining it.

Why Stability Requires Constant Adjustment

A paradox that's central to understanding the wobble is that staying on course requires constant course correction. Think about riding a bicycle. You're never perfectly balanced. You're constantly making micro-adjustments with a slight shift in weight, a tiny turn of the handlebars just to maintain balance. If you tried to lock the handlebars in a perfectly straight position, you'd immediately fall over.

> *The appearance of stability is actually the result of continuous adjustment.*

The same is true in discipleship. The conditions are never static.

Your circumstances change. New job, new city, new relationships, new health challenges. What worked in one season doesn't work in the next. The spiritual practices that sustained you when you were single might not translate to life with young children. The giving pattern that felt generous when you were debt-free feels different when you're contributing to the care of aging parents.

You change. Your understanding matures and your capacity grows or shrinks as you move through life. What you once needed you might outgrow. What you once dismissed might become essential. The questions that gripped you at twenty-five might be resolved by forty, but new questions emerge.

Your relationship with God deepens. As you grow in intimacy with God, you see things you couldn't see before. You become aware of patterns you didn't know were there. What looked like faithfulness at one level of maturity looks like compromise at the next level. This isn't condemnation it's an indicator of growth and it requiring adjustment.

The broader culture shifts. The challenges your grandparents faced in living faithfully aren't identical to yours. New questions arise, new temptations emerge, new opportunities open as our culture shifts. Faithfulness in your Christian walk will require discernment that your life prior to belief in Christ didn't require.

> To stay on course through cultural shifts, you will always have to keep adjusting.

Fixed Points vs. Fluid Practices

So how do you navigate? How do you maintain direction while making constant adjustments? You need to distinguish between fixed points and fluid practices.

Fixed Points - What Doesn't Move: These are your navigational references, the truths and principles that remain constant regardless of your circumstances. They're how you orient yourself when everything else is in flux. For a Christian, fixed points include:

- The character of God as revealed in Scripture and, supremely, in Jesus.
- The gospel: the life, death, and resurrection of Jesus Christ.
- Your identity as a child of God, adopted and deeply loved.
- The call to love God with your whole life and love your neighbor as yourself.
- The reality of the Kingdom of God, both now and to come.
- The presence and guidance of the Holy Spirit.
- The authority of Scripture as God's revelation to mankind.
- The community of faith as the body of Christ.

These don't change. They're not up for negotiation. They're your North Star, your lighthouse, your GPS coordinates.

Fluid Practices - What Adapts: These are the specific ways you live out the fixed points in your current circumstances. They're the "how" that serves the "what." They should absolutely change as conditions change. Fluid practices include:

- The specific rhythm and content of your prayer life.
- The particular spiritual disciplines you emphasize in a given season.
- How you structure your time, resources, and relationships.
- The ministries or service opportunities you engage.
- Your approach to fasting, Sabbath, solitude, and study.
- The balance between engagement and withdrawal from culture.
- The level of risk you take in obedience.
- How you navigate specific relational dynamics.

These should flex, and they're context-dependent. What works for someone else might not work for you. What worked for you last year might not work this year.

> The wobble happens when you're adjusting your practices (fluid) in response to circumstances while keeping your orientation to the fixed points constant.

Recognizing Your Pattern

Here's where self-awareness becomes crucial - everyone has a wobble pattern. Understanding yours helps you navigate more effectively.

Some people wobble toward certainty. When things get uncertain, they tighten their grip on doctrine, become more rigid in their practices, and seek more clarity and definition. This can be healthy as a way to stay grounded in truth when everything feels unstable. But it can also become unhealthy using certainty as a shield against mystery, demanding answers God isn't currently providing, and judging others who live with more ambiguity in their lives.

Some people wobble toward doubt. When things get difficult, they question everything, hold convictions loosely, emphasize mystery over clarity. This can be healthy by staying humble, remaining open, and avoiding the arrogance of false certainty. But it can also become unhealthy in using doubt as an excuse to avoid commitment, refusing to stand for anything, thus creating instability for yourself and others.

Some people wobble toward zeal. When they encounter truth, they want to act immediately and radically. This can be healthy in responding to the Spirit's promptings, being willing to pay the cost of obedience, and moving forward in faith. But it can also become unhealthy in creating burning out, acting presumptuously or leaving wreckage in their wake.

Some people wobble toward wisdom (or what they call wisdom). When they sense a call to action, they want to think, plan, consider, wait. This can be healthy in being wise as serpents, counting the cost, and avoiding foolish mistakes. But it can also become unhealthy creating analysis paralysis, fear disguised as prudence, or using "wisdom" to justify disobedience.

Most of us tend toward one side of each tension. Knowing your pattern helps you recognize when you're over-correcting and need to adjust.

The Difference Between Wobble and Drift

Now we come a critical distinction - how do you know if you're navigating or just drifting?

Wobble is characterized by:

- *Awareness.* You know where you are. You're honest about your current state in seeing the struggles, the doubts, and the tensions. You're not pretending things are different than they are.
- *Intention.* You know where you're headed. You have a direction, even if the path isn't perfectly clear. You're moving toward something, not just away from something.
- *Engagement.* You're actively steering. You're making choices, seeking counsel, responding to feedback, and adjusting based on what you're learning. You're not passive.
- *Reference points.* You're checking your position relative to fixed points. You're reading Scripture, engaging with community, listening for the Spirit's voice, and evaluating your choices against your convictions.
- *Course correction.* When you realize you've drifted off course, you adjust. You repent (which literally means "change direction"), you re calibrate, and get back on track.

Drift is characterized by:

- *Numbness.* You're not really aware of where you are. You're going through motions, telling yourself you're fine, and avoiding honest self-

assessment.
- *Aimlessness.* You don't have a clear direction. You're just responding to immediate pressures and pleasures, carried by whatever current is strongest.
- *Passivity.* You're not actively steering. Things are happening to you rather than you engaging or adjusting to them. You're reactive rather than responsive.
- *Lost reference points.* You've stopped checking your position. Scripture reading has fallen away, community connection has weakened, prayer has become sporadic or nonexistent. You're navigating by feelings alone.
- *No correction.* When you notice you're off course, you either don't care or you justify it. You rationalize rather than repent and continue moving in the same direction even though you know it's wrong.

<u>Here's a real world concrete example:</u>

Wobble: You're struggling with your prayer life. You used to pray every morning, but it's felt dry for months. You're honest about this struggle and mention it to your small group. You read about different approaches to prayer and try some new practices. Some work, some don't. You keep showing up even when it feels mechanical because you trust that practice matters even when the feeling is absent. You're navigating.

Drift: You're struggling with your prayer life. You used to pray every morning, but it's felt dry for months. So you just... stop. You tell yourself you'll get back to it when it feels meaningful again. Months pass. You don't mention it to anyone because you're vaguely ashamed but not enough to actually change anything. You rationalize that God knows your heart anyway, so formal prayer isn't really necessary. You've drifted.

> *See the difference? The external circumstance (dry prayer life) is the same. But the internal posture is completely different.*

Warning Signs - When Wobble Becomes Drift

How do you know if you've crossed the line from healthy navigation to passive drift? Here are some warning signs:

- *You've stopped being honest.* With yourself, with God, with others. You're managing image rather than dealing with reality.
- *You've lost your reference points.* You can't remember the last time you seriously engaged with Scripture, experienced meaningful community, or evaluated your life against your stated convictions.
- *You're justifying rather than repenting.* When you notice you're off course, your first move is to explain why it's okay rather than to change direction.
- *You're isolated.* You've pulled away from the people who would ask you hard questions or speak truth into your life.
- *You're numb.* You're going through the motions but not feeling much of anything—not conviction, not doubt, not zeal, not even struggle. Just numbness.
- *You can't articulate where you're headed.* If someone asked you what you're aiming for in your spiritual life, you'd have no clear answer.
- *You've stopped course-correcting.* You notice you're drifting but you don't do anything about it. Days become weeks become months.

> If you recognize these signs in yourself, there's the great news in that awareness is the first step back to navigation. The fact that you can see the drift means you're not completely lost. You can still find your fixed points and start steering again.

Embracing the Wobble

The wobble isn't something to eliminate. It's something to navigate well. You're not going to reach a point in your discipleship where you've "arrived" and no longer need to make adjustments. You're not going to achieve a perfect balance where the tensions resolve and the navigation becomes effortless.

This side of eternity, you're always going to be wobbling and feeling the pull of competing desires, navigating complex circumstances, adjusting your course in response to changing conditions. The goal isn't to stop the wobble. The goal is to wobble well—to navigate with awareness, intention, and reference to fixed points. To stay engaged in the process of steering rather than passively drifting. To make course corrections when needed rather than pretending you're still on track when you're not.

The harbor pilot doesn't apologize for all the course corrections. They're not seen as failures or weaknesses. They're part of the job. They're what makes safe passage possible. Your wobble is the same. It's not a malfunction in your discipleship, but, rather, it's how discipleship actually works.

> So the question isn't: "How do I stop wobbling?"
>
> The question is: "How do I recognize my pattern, maintain my reference points, and steer toward Christ through whatever conditions I'm currently navigating?"
>
> *That's what we're going to explore in the next section—the practical framework for navigating the wobble well.*

5

Recognizing Your Pattern

You can't navigate what you can't see. There is a fundamental problem most Christians face in their discipleship. It's that they're wobbling with constant course correction, responding to tensions, and adjusting their practices but they're doing it unconsciously. They don't recognize their own patterns, so they can't learn from them, can't anticipate them, and can't distinguish between healthy navigation and destructive drift.

They're steering blind.

Self-awareness isn't vanity. It's not narcissistic navel-gazing or an excuse for endless introspection. In the context of discipleship, self-awareness is a navigation tool being one of the most important tools you have.

You need to know how you specifically tend to wobble. What tensions pull you most strongly? What are your default responses under pressure? Where do you consistently over-correct? What blind spots keep you from seeing clearly? Without this knowledge, you're navigating by feel in the dark, hoping you don't crash into something before you figure out where you are.

Your Personal Wobble Signature

Every disciple has a wobble signature, which is a recognizable pattern in how they respond to spiritual tensions and navigate discipleship challenges. Think of it like a fingerprint or a handwriting style. No two are exactly alike, but there are identifiable patterns and tendencies that show up consistently across situations.

Some of this is temperament and the way you're naturally wired. Some of it is based on the history of experiences that have shaped your understanding of God and yourself. Some of it is current context in the season of life you're in and the pressures you're under. All of it creates a pattern. Understanding your signature means you can:

Anticipate your responses. When a new tension or challenge emerges, you have a pretty good idea how you'll be tempted to respond. This gives you the opportunity to pause and choose rather than just reacting.

Recognize when you're over-correcting. Every strength pushed too far becomes a weakness. If you know your natural lean, you can catch yourself when you're leaning too far.

Ask for specific help. Instead of generic prayer requests or vague accountability, you can tell people exactly where you need eyes on your life and what warning signs to watch for.

Make wiser choices. You can structure your life in ways that support your growth areas and put guardrails around your vulnerable areas.

Let's look at what this looks like in practice.

Mapping Your Tensions

Remember the three core tensions we identified: Conviction/Compromise, Certainty/Doubt, and Zeal/Wisdom. Understanding your wobble signature means identifying where you naturally land on each of these continuums and how you tend to move when things get difficult.

The Conviction/Compromise Continuum

Some people lean naturally toward conviction. These are the "hold the line" disciples. When faced with competing values or complex situations, their instinct is to stand firm on principle. They'd rather be right than comfortable. They're willing to pay social costs to maintain integrity. They see compromise as the greater danger.

Their strength: They have clear boundaries. They won't be easily swayed by cultural pressure or social convenience. They take Scripture seriously and aren't afraid to be counter-cultural.

Their vulnerability: They can become rigid, judgmental, and disconnected from reality. They might prioritize being "right" over being loving. They can mistake their cultural preferences for biblical mandates. They struggle to extend grace to people who don't share their convictions.

Other people lean naturally toward compromise. These are the "build bridges" disciples. When faced with tension, their instinct is to find common ground, to accommodate, and to keep relationships intact. They'd rather be gracious than rigid. They're willing to flex on secondary issues to maintain unity. They see divisiveness as the greater danger.

Their strength: They can navigate complexity well. They extend grace easily. They can relate to people across differences. They don't make mountains out of molehills. They create space for people to journey toward truth rather than demanding immediate conformity.

Their vulnerability: They can lose their distinctiveness. They might prioritize keeping peace over speaking truth. They can rationalize away convictions that become inconvenient. They may struggle to draw necessary lines or take costly stands.

Where do you fall on this continuum?

When you face a situation where your convictions clash with your circumstances, what's your first instinct? To hold firm or to flex? To prioritize truth or relationship? To risk being seen as rigid or as compromised? And, of critical importance, you know when you're leaning too far in your natural direction?

The Certainty/Doubt Continuum

Some people lean naturally toward certainty. These are the "anchor down" disciples. When faith gets difficult, their instinct is to double down on what they know to be true. They emphasize God's promises, recall His past faithfulness, stand on Scripture. They see doubt as the enemy to be resisted.

Their strength: They provide stability for themselves and others. They can speak truth with confidence when everyone else is wavering. They're less likely to be blown around by every new idea or emotional fluctuation. They can lead with conviction.

Their vulnerability: They can become brittle and unable to hold mystery or ambiguity. They might dismiss legitimate questions as "just doubt." They can weaponize certainty against people who are genuinely struggling. They might confuse confidence in their interpretation with confidence in God.

Other people lean naturally toward doubt. These are the "hold it loosely" disciples. When faith gets difficult, their instinct is to question, to acknowledge complexity, and to sit with mystery. They emphasize God's transcendence beyond our understanding. They see false certainty as the greater danger.

Their strength: They remain humble. They can hold space for hard questions without forcing premature answers. They're less likely to mistake their theology for God Himself. They can relate to people in the wilderness of doubt because they've been there.

Their vulnerability: They can become untethered with no firm ground to stand on. They might use doubt as a shield against commitment. They can create instability for themselves and others. They might confuse humility with perpetual indecision.

Where do you fall on this continuum?

When your faith is tested through suffering, through intellectual challenge, through spiritual dryness, what's your instinct? To grip tighter to what you believe or to hold everything more loosely? To emphasize what you know or what you don't? And when do you know you're leaning too far in your natural direction?

The Zeal/Wisdom Continuum

Some people lean naturally toward zeal. These are the "all in" disciples. When they encounter truth or sense God's leading, their instinct is to act immediately and radically. They'll reorganize their entire life around a new conviction. They're willing to take risks. They see caution as the enemy of faith.

Their strength: They move forward. They don't experience paralysis by analysis. They respond to the Spirit's promptings without endless deliberation. They're willing to pay costs others aren't. They create momentum.

Their vulnerability: They can burn out or burn others. They might mistake their passion for God's specific leading. They can be impulsive, making commitments they can't sustain. They might judge others who are more measured. They can leave relational wreckage in their wake.

Other people lean naturally toward wisdom. These are the "count the cost" disciples. When they sense a call to action, their instinct is to evaluate, plan, consider implications, and seek counsel. They want to move forward thoughtfully. They may see impulsiveness as the enemy of faithfulness.

Their strength: They make sustainable choices. They consider second and third-order effects or down the road implications. They're less likely to crash and burn. They can offer valuable perspective to zealous people who need it. They build things that last.

Their vulnerability: They can become paralyzed, never quite ready to move. They might mistake fear for prudence. They can rationalize away costly obedience. They might judge others who take risks they're not willing to take. They may miss opportunities that require quick response.

Where do you fall on this continuum?

When you encounter a new truth or sense a call to change, what's your instinct? To act now or to wait and consider? To trust your passion or to test it? To move boldly or carefully? And when do you know you're leaning too far in your natural direction?

Your Default Under Pressure

Recognizing your pattern is critical. You don't just have a natural lean, you also have a default setting that kicks in under pressure. When life gets hard, when you're stressed, when you're exhausted, when you're overwhelmed, the tendency is that you don't carefully navigate the tensions. You revert to your default.

- If you naturally lean toward conviction, pressure pushes you into rigidity.
- If you naturally lean toward compromise, pressure pushes you into people-pleasing.
- If you naturally lean toward certainty, pressure pushes you into false confidence.
- If you naturally lean toward doubt, pressure pushes you into cynicism.
- If you naturally lean toward zeal, pressure pushes you into recklessness.
- If you naturally lean toward wisdom, pressure pushes you into paralysis.

This is when you need self-awareness most, yet it's also when you're least likely to have it. The pressure narrows your vision. You can't see that you're over-correcting. You're just surviving. So you need to know your default *before* you're under pressure. You need to have identified it in calm waters so you can recognize it in the storm.

Questions to identify your default: Think about the last time you were really stressed—maybe a crisis at work, a relational conflict, a health scare, financial pressure, or a family crisis. How did you respond spiritually?

- Did you become more rigid or more flexible?
- Did you grip your beliefs tighter or question everything?
- Did you act impulsively or freeze completely?
- Did you isolate or seek support?
- Did you double down on spiritual disciplines or abandon them?
- Did you become judgmental of others or lose all conviction yourself?

Your answers reveal your default. And your default reveals where you're most vulnerable to drift.

The Difference Between Productive Wobble and Destructive Drift

Now we get to the practical heart of this chapter. How do you know if your wobbling is productive navigation or destructive drift?

- Both involve movement.
- Both involve tension.
- Both can feel uncomfortable and uncertain.

So how do you tell them apart?

Productive Wobble Has Direction

When you're wobbling productively, there's overall forward movement even if the path isn't straight. Over time, months and years, you can look back and see that you've grown, that you're more Christ-like than you were, that you understand yourself and God more deeply. The wobble hasn't been random. It's been navigation through real conditions toward a real destination.

Destructive drift, on the other hand, has no net direction. You're just moving. You might be busy, active, even exhausted from all the motion. But when you look back, you haven't moved forward. You're no closer to Christ than you were. You've just been spinning.

Productive Wobble Maintains Connection

When you're wobbling productively, you stay engaged with God, with Scripture, with community, and with yourself. You might be struggling, but you're struggling *in relationship*. You're bringing your doubt to God, your questions to trusted people, and your confusion to Scripture. The wobble happens in the context of connection.

Destructive drift isolates. You pull away from the people and practices that would help you navigate. You stop being honest about where you are. You disconnect from your reference points. You're wobbling, but you're wobbling alone, which means you have no perspective on whether your course corrections are actually corrections or just more drift.

Productive Wobble Includes Correction

When you're wobbling productively, you're willing to adjust when you realize you're off course. Someone speaks truth into your life, and you receive it. You recognize a pattern that's not serving you, and you change it. You see that you've leaned too far in one direction, and you self-correct. You're actively steering, which means you're willing to change direction when needed.

Destructive drift resists correction. You rationalize, defend, and justify. When people express concern, you dismiss them. When Scripture convicts you, you explain it away. When you sense the Spirit's prompting to change, you ignore it. You're committed to your current trajectory even when it's not working, which means you're not actually navigating, you're just insisting on continuing the direction you're already heading.

Productive Wobble Creates Growth

When you're wobbling productively, the process itself transforms you. The tensions make you wiser. The course corrections teach you about yourself and God. The mistakes become lessons. The struggles deepen your faith rather than eroding it. You're being formed through the process.

Destructive drift creates damage. The wobbling wears you down. The tensions exhaust you. The mistakes compound. The struggles harden you or make you cynical. You're being worn away rather than built up.

Productive Wobble Has Accountability

When you're wobbling productively, other people can see what you're doing and speak into it. You're open about your struggles and your process. You invite input. You give people permission to ask hard questions. You're navigating in community.

Destructive drift hides. You manage your image. You keep people at arm's length. You're selective about what you share, always presenting the version of yourself that looks like you have it together. You're protecting yourself from the very accountability that could help you navigate better.

Warning Signs - When Wobble Becomes Wandering

Here are some specific questions to ask yourself and the red flags that indicate you've crossed from healthy wobble into destructive drift:

Is Your Gap Is Growing?

Remember the gap we talked about in Chapter 2 as being the distance between who you present yourself to be and who you actually are? If that gap is widening rather than narrowing, if you're spending more energy managing your image and less energy actually growing, that's drift.

Productive wobble narrows the gap over time. You become more integrated, more congruent. The Sunday version and the Monday version start to look more alike, not because you've perfected the Sunday version, but because you've become more honest about the Monday version and more committed to addressing it.

Have You Lost Your Appetite?

When you're wobbling productively, even if things are hard, you still have spiritual appetite. You still want to connect with God, even if the connection feels thin. You still value Scripture, even if it's not speaking to you clearly right now. You still hunger for growth, even if you're frustrated with your pace.

When you're drifting, you lose your appetite. You don't really care about prayer anymore. Scripture feels irrelevant. Growth feels like too much work. You're spiritually apathetic simply going through minimal motions to maintain appearances but with no real desire underneath.

Are You Defending Your Position?

When you're wobbling productively, you're open to input. You might not immediately accept every piece of advice, but you're willing to consider it. You ask questions like: "Am I seeing this clearly?" "What am I missing?" "Where might I be wrong?"

When you're drifting, you're defensive. Criticism, even gentle, loving criticism, triggers justification. You explain why your choices make sense. You point out why the other person doesn't understand your situation. You're more interested in being understood than in understanding.

Are You Comfortable?

This one is counter-intuitive, *productive wobble is usually uncomfortable*. You're navigating tensions, making hard choices, denying yourself things you want, and pushing yourself to grow. There's friction.

Destructive drift, paradoxically, can feel comfortable, at least initially. You've settled into patterns that require minimal effort. You're not wrestling with hard questions because you've stopped asking them. You're not experiencing conviction because you've learned to tune it out.

> If your spiritual life has become entirely comfortable—no tension, no struggle, no challenge—that's not peace. That's numbness. And numbness is drift.

Has Your Story Stopped?

When you're wobbling productively, your story is ongoing. You have things to say when people ask how you're growing. Not performance updates - "I'm reading through the Bible in a year!" - but real story. "I'm learning this about myself." "God is teaching me this lesson." "I'm wrestling with this question."

Your story should be alive.

When you're drifting, your story has stopped. When people ask about your spiritual life, you reference old stories about the things God did years ago, breakthroughs from past seasons. You don't have anything current to share because nothing current is happening. You're living off yesterday's bread.

Course Correction - Getting Back to Navigation

If you recognize drift in yourself or if you've read this chapter and realized you've been wandering rather than wobbling, here's the good news; *you can start navigating again right now.*

The awareness itself is the first step. Drift is only truly dangerous when you don't realize it's happening. Once you see it, you can respond to it. Here's how to get back to active navigation:

Get Honest

Stop managing your image. Tell someone (a trusted friend, a mentor, a counselor) where you actually are not where you wish you were or where you're supposed to be. Where you are. This is terrifying for most people, but it's essential. *You can't navigate from a fictional position. You need to start with reality.*

Reconnect with Your Fixed Points

If you've drifted away from Scripture, community, and/or prayer, actively engage and reconnect. Not with some massive overhaul or ambitious plan, just reconnect. Read one Psalm. Reach out to one person. Pray one honest prayer. *Get your reference points back in view so you can orient yourself.*

Ask for Accountability

Give specific people specific permission to ask you specific questions. Don't say "Pray for me" or "Keep me accountable." It's always better to be specific, such as "Ask me every week if I've been honest with my spouse about our finances." "Check in with me monthly about whether I'm still avoiding that conversation I need to have." *Make your accountability request specific and concrete so you can't dodge it.*

Make One Course Correction

Don't try to fix everything at once. Identify one specific area where you've drifted and make one specific correction. Focus on one behavior to change, one pattern to interrupt, or one commitment to keep. Start steering again, even if it's just one small adjustment. Navigation is a practice. *You rebuild a skill by exercising it.*

Expect Discomfort

When you start actively navigating again after a period of drift, it's going to feel hard. The muscles have atrophied. The practices feel awkward. The tensions you've been avoiding will suddenly be right in front of you again. That discomfort is good. It means you're engaged again. It means you're wobbling productively rather than drifting passively. Don't mistake the discomfort for evidence that you're doing something wrong. *It's evidence that you're doing something right.*

Your Pattern Is Not Your Prison

One final word before we move on. Knowing your pattern or your natural lean, your default under pressure, and your vulnerabilities is not about resignation. Nor is it, "Well, I guess I'll always struggle with this, so I might as well accept it."

Your pattern is not your prison. It's your map.

It tells you where to pay attention, where to build in support, where to invite accountability, and where to expect challenges. It helps you navigate more skillfully, not navigate less. You're not trying to eliminate your pattern or become someone with a different signature. You're trying to recognize your pattern so you can work with it rather than being unconsciously controlled by it.

The harbor pilot doesn't fight against the ship's natural handling characteristics he or she learns how to work with them. They know this vessel turns slowly, so they start the turn earlier. They know this ship responds sluggishly in reverse, so he or she plans accordingly. That's what you're doing. You are learning your vessel, understanding how you respond. You are anticipating your tendencies so you can navigate them intentionally.

> The wobble is inevitable. But whether it becomes productive navigation or destructive drift—that's largely in your hands.

> *Now let's talk about the framework that makes productive wobble possible.*

III

The Framework for Forward Momentum

6

The Pilocon Principles

You can't navigate without fixed points. We've established that the wobble is normal and that course correction is how discipleship actually works. We've identified the tensions you'll constantly navigate and the patterns you need to recognize in yourself. A crucial question is, what keeps you from wobbling off course entirely?

What prevents productive navigation from becoming destructive drift?

You need principles, not rules. You don't need a rigid system that dictates every decision but fixed points that orient you when everything else is in flux. I call these the Pilocon Principles, and they're built on a foundation that's been tested through my own wobbling discipleship journey.

> I am responsible for my actions and my attitudes and nothing else is a personal principle I try to live by.

The Core Foundation - Two Things Under Your Control

In your entire life, you control exactly two things - your actions and your attitudes. That's it, just two.

- You don't control your circumstances.
- You don't control other people's behavior.
- You don't control the economy, the weather, your health challenges, or whether that opportunity comes through.
- You don't control how people respond to you, what they think about you, or whether they keep their commitments to you.

You control your actions which are your responses to what happens in your life. You control your attitudes in how you choose to frame and interpret what you experience. This might sound limiting at first. It might feel like I'm telling you that you're powerless. But it's actually the opposite. Understanding what you control and what you don't is the most freeing realization you can have as a disciple. When you stop trying to control things outside of your control, you stop wasting energy on futile efforts. When you accept full responsibility for the things you do control, you stop making excuses and start making progress.

> Learning this is the core foundation everything else is built on.

Every other principle flows from the one core truth that I am responsible for my actions and attitudes. I cannot blame my circumstances, my past, other people, or even "how God made me." I own my responses. I own my choices. I own my growth.

Principle 1: Take Responsibility Before Response

Something happens in your life - a difficulty, a conflict, a challenge and most people's first instinct is to respond, react, explain, defend, or justify. Taking responsibility means that you first pause before responding and ask yourself:

What am I responsible for in this situation?
  Not

- "Who's at fault?"
- "Who started this?"
- "Is this fair?"

Rather

- "What do I control here?"
- "What are my actions?"
- "What is my attitude?"

This principle keeps you from playing the blame game. It prevents you from positioning yourself as a victim of your circumstances. It forces you to own your part even when your part is small, even when the other person's part is larger, even when the situation wasn't your fault.

Let me give you a concrete example from my own life: Years ago I was let go from a position that I believed God had clearly led me to take. I had uprooted my family, moved to a new state, and within a relatively short time, the job ended badly. My first instinct was to focus on what *they* did wrong—the leadership failures, the broken promises, the unfair treatment. And some of that was real. There were legitimate grievances. But taking responsibility first meant I had to ask a series of questions such as. "What was *my* part?" "What were my actions?" "What was *my* attitude?"

The answers were uncomfortable as I had allowed bitterness to grow. I had withdrawn rather than communicating clearly. I had made assumptions rather than asking questions. I had let my expectations dictate my responses rather than assessing the actual situation. I couldn't control any of the people involved in the decision to fire me. I could only control my actions and attitudes.

Taking responsibility first meant I dealt with my part before I addressed anything else. It meant I repented where I needed to repent. It meant I learned what I needed to learn. It meant I adjusted my actions and attitudes before I ever tried to correct someone else's.

Application:

When something goes wrong in your life such as in your marriage, your job, your ministry, or your relationships, your first question should always be "What am I responsible for here?" Not to beat yourself up. Not to take blame that isn't yours. But to own what is yours before you do anything else.

> This principle keeps your wobble from becoming drift. When you take responsibility first, you're actively navigating on your life's journey. You're steering. You're engaged.

Principle 2: Seek Authenticity Over Performance

Authenticity is the antidote to the performance gap in our lives that was discussed earlier between pew and practice.

- *Authenticity means you're the same person* in every context. Not that you act identically in every situation—you'll naturally adjust your communication style, your energy level, your topics of conversation based on context. But your core self remains consistent. You're not performing one version of yourself on Sunday and living as a different person on Monday.
- *Authenticity means you're honest* about where you actually are in your journey, not where you wish you were or where you think you should be.
- *Authenticity means you admit* your struggles, acknowledge your doubts, confess your failures—not as a performance of vulnerability, but as a practice of truth-telling.

You can't course-correct from a position you're not actually in. If you're pretending to be somewhere you're not, you can't make the adjustments you actually need. Think about it in sailing terms. If you tell yourself you're headed due north when you're actually headed northeast, your course corrections will be wrong. You'll keep adjusting based on false information, and you'll never actually reach your destination.

> *Authenticity in discipleship means you assess your actual position honestly so you can navigate from where you truly are, not from where you're pretending to be, to grow in your discipleship.*

Application:

Stop managing your image. Start telling the truth to yourself, to God, and to trusted people in your life. When someone asks how you're doing spiritually, don't give the Sunday morning answer. Give the Monday reality answer. When you're in small group and the question is asked about your spiritual practices, don't describe your ideal or your intentions. Describe your actual reality. When you're evaluating your growth, don't compare yourself to some imagined standard of where you "should" be. Look at where you actually are and where you're actually moving.

> This doesn't mean you broadcast every struggle to everyone. Wisdom still applies. But within your circle of discipleship relationships, authenticity has to trump performance.

Principle 3: Value the Process Over Arrival

This principle directly addresses the straight line myth. If you're oriented toward "arrival"—toward reaching some destination where you've "made it" spiritually, you will be perpetually disappointed. You'll judge every wobble as a failure. You'll see every course correction as evidence that something's wrong. But if you're striving toward process and going toward the ongoing work of navigation, growth, and formation, then the wobble makes sense. The course corrections are expected. The journey itself becomes the point.

I've been following Christ for decades, and I'm still wobbling. I'm still making course corrections. I'm still learning things about myself that need to change. I'm still being surprised by areas of immaturity I didn't realize were there.

This isn't failure. This is process.

Paul, at the end of his life, with all his ministry accomplishments and theological brilliance, wrote: "Not that I have already obtained this or am already perfect, but I press on to make it my own, because Christ Jesus has made me his own" (Philippians 3:12). Paul was oriented toward process, not arrival. He was pressing on, not claiming to have arrived.

> *This principle keeps you from the exhaustion of feeling that you're constantly failing and the shame of never measuring up. You should not be trying to reach some static destination. You should be engaged in dynamic process.*

Application:

Stop asking: "Have I arrived yet?" Start asking: "Am I engaged in the process? Am I moving? Am I responding to correction? Am I learning?"

Celebrate progress without demanding perfection. Notice growth without claiming completion. When you catch yourself comparing your current state to some imagined "mature Christian" state, redirect your actions and attitudes. Instead, compare your current maturity to your maturity six months ago, a year ago, five years ago. Are you continually growing? That's what matters.

> The process is the point. The navigation is the work. The wobble is the signature of a life being actively formed by the Holy Spirit in our discipleship journey.

Principle 4: Focus on Preparation Over Prediction

This principle addresses our tendency to want to know the future, to have everything mapped out, to predict where God is taking us before we take a step. But prediction invites paralysis. When you're trying to predict outcomes, you're setting expectations that may not align with God's actual plan. You're creating measurements of success that might not be His measurements. You're projecting a future that may not be the future He has for you.

Preparation, on the other hand, positions you to move with the Spirit wherever He leads.

Preparation means you're doing the consistent work of discipleship through reading Scripture, praying, engaging community, and practicing spiritual disciplines, not because you know exactly where it's leading, but because these practices prepare you to respond when God moves in your life. Preparation means you're developing your capacity to hear the Holy Spirit's voice, discern His leading, and obey His promptings, even when you can't see the full picture.

I've had so many experiences where I tried to predict what God was doing, only to have Him do something completely different. The prediction created expectation. The unmet expectation created disappointment. The disappointment made it harder to see what God was actually doing.

I have to focus on preparation instead of predicting the future so that I simply do the next thing He's clearly shown me, stay consistent in the basics, and position myself to be available. Only then am I ready to move when He moves, even if it's in a direction I never predicted.

Application:
Stop trying to figure out God's complete plan for your life. Stop demanding to see the full map before you take a step. Instead, ask: "What has He clearly shown me to do right now? What's the next faithful step?" Then take it. And prepare yourself through consistent practices to take the next step after that

when He reveals it.

> Your job as a Christ follower is not to predict. Your job is to prepare and obey.

Principle 5: Prioritize Consistency Over Intensity

I learned this principle the hard way through athletics. I've been a weekend athlete my whole life—running, cycling, triathlons, racquetball. And I've repeatedly made the same mistake of getting fired up about an event, training intensely for a short period, then burning out or getting injured.

> *One great workout doesn't win a race. Thirty to forty good workouts strung together in close proximity – that's what wins races. The same is true in discipleship. One intense spiritual experience doesn't produce maturity. Consistent, steady engagement over time – that's what produces growth.*

We're often drawn to intensity. The powerful worship service. The transformative retreat. The breakthrough moment in prayer. These are good. These can be genuine encounters with God. But if you're only seeking intensity or if you're only engaged when the feelings are strong and the experience is powerful, you will wobble wildly on your discipleship journey. You'll have dramatic highs followed by dramatic lows. Emotional intensity should not be mistaken for spiritual growth.

Consistency is what produces actual change. Consistent time in Scripture even when it doesn't feel transformative. Consistent prayer even when it feels dry. Consistent community even when it's ordinary. Consistent obedience even when it's mundane.

> *This is how your wobble amplitude decreases over time. It happens not*

through occasional intense course corrections, but through consistent small adjustments.

Application:

Build sustainable rhythms, not heroic efforts it's better to read Scripture for 15 minutes every day than to do a marathon Bible reading session once a month with nothing in between. It's better to have brief, consistent prayers throughout each day than to attend one annual prayer retreat. It's better to have weekly meaningful conversations within your small group than only occasional deep confessionals with a leader and no follow-up. Ask yourself: "What can I sustain?" "What can I do consistently, not just when I'm motivated?"

> Develop the muscle of consistency in your spiritual walk. Never let the pursuit of intensity undermine the power of consistency.

Principle 6: Choose Community Over Independence

You cannot navigate your Christian walk well alone. The harbor pilot doesn't navigate solo. He or she is in constant communication with the harbormaster, with other vessels, and with support systems such as radar, GPS, charts, and communication technology. They don't rely solely on their own perception.

The harbor pilot cannot rely only on what he or she sees - neither should you.

The American church has absorbed too much individualism from the surrounding culture. We treat faith as a personal, private matter. We make discipleship about "me and Jesus." We pursue spiritual growth as a solo project. But that's not how discipleship works in Scripture. It's always communal. The letters of the New Testament are written to communities, not individuals. The "one another" Biblical commands reinforce the idea that you should be in close relationship with other believers. The imagery of the body of Christ speaks to the fact that interdependence with other believers and community are essential for navigation.

- *You need other people to see your blind spots.* You can't see your own patterns clearly. You need people who know you well enough to point out when you're drifting.
- *You need other people to speak truth when you're rationalizing.* Your own internal dialogue will always be self-justifying. You need external voices who love you enough to challenge you.
- *You need other people to encourage you when you want to quit.* The journey is long. You will have seasons of discouragement. You need people who can remind you of truth when you've lost sight of it.
- *You need other people to celebrate with you when you grow.* Growth is meant to be shared. When you experience a breakthrough, when you make progress, when you see God work—you need people who will rejoice with you.

Christian community isn't optional. It is essential.

Application:

Stop trying to navigate alone and treating discipleship as a private pursuit. Find your people. These are not casual church acquaintances. Seek out actual discipleship relationships - people you're in consistent, honest, mutual relationship with. Give them permission to ask hard questions by giving them access to your actual life, not just your Sunday version. Meet regularly, weekly if possible, not for Bible study alone, but for doing life together. Have honest conversation about your actual struggles, your actual growth, your actual wobble. And be sure to reciprocate by speaking into their lives too.

> You're not just receiving input—you're giving it. You're speaking truth into their lives as they speak truth into yours.

The Integration - How the Principles Work Together

These six principles work together as a navigation system:

- *Responsibility before response* keeps you from blame and victim hood.
- *Authenticity over performance* ensures you're navigating from your actual position, not a fictional one.
- *Process over arrival* reframes the wobble as an expected part of your journey rather than constant failure.
- *Preparation over prediction* positions you to move with God rather than trying to predict His plans.
- *Consistency over intensity* builds sustainable growth rather than dramatic spikes and crashes.
- *Community over independence* provides the external reference points, relationships and accountability you need as you grow spiritually.

Together these principles create a framework for productively navigating your wobble. They don't eliminate the tensions. You will still navigate conviction and compromise, certainty and doubt, zeal and wisdom. But they give you fixed points to reference as you navigate those tensions. They keep you oriented toward Christ even when your path isn't straight. They help you distinguish between a productive wobble and a destructive drift. They provide a way to assess your discipleship that isn't based on performance or comparison, but on actual growth.

Living the Principles

These aren't rules to follow rigidly. They're principles to apply wisely. Sometimes one principle will be more relevant than others in a given situation. Sometimes they'll be in tension with each other and you'll need to discern which to prioritize.

The key is to internalize them. Make them part of how you think, not just what you do. Let them shape your instincts so that when you're under pressure, when you're wobbling hard, these principles can guide your course corrections almost automatically.

This takes time, practice and consistency, but it's worth it. These principles don't just help you navigate the wobble, they help you embrace it. They help you see it not as failure but as faithfulness, and not as weakness but as the way Christian discipleship actually works.

You're can't stop wobbling, but you can wobble well.

And that starts with owning these principles as your own.

7

Tools for the Journey

Principles tell you *what* to aim for and tools help you *how* to get there. The Pilocon Principles we just explored are your fixed points which provide the constants to orient you when everything else is shifting. But principles alone don't move you forward. You need practices and rhythms. You need actual tools you can use to navigate the wobble.

Tools are not the same as systems.

Systems promise control. They offer step-by-step processes that guarantee results if you just follow them correctly. They turn discipleship into a project with milestones, metrics, and completion dates. Tools, on the other hand, acknowledge that you're navigating dynamic conditions. They're instruments that help you respond to what's actually happening, not prescriptions that dictate what should happen.

Harbor pilots do not follow a rigid system instead they use tools. Charts, radar, communication equipment, their own experience and training are the tools of choice. The pilot adapts how he or she uses these tools based on current conditions. The tools serve the navigation; they don't replace it. There are also tools to assist you as you navigate your discipleship journey.

Fixed Points vs. Fluid Practices

Before we dive into specific tools, we need to revisit and deepen a distinction that's essential for navigating well - the difference between fixed points and fluid practices as covered earlier in this book.

Fixed Points: What Doesn't Move

These are the non-negotiables in your Christian walk and are truths and realities that remain constant regardless of your circumstances, your season of life, or your current struggles. For a disciple of Christ, fixed points include:

- The character of God as revealed in Scripture and supremely in Jesus Christ.
- The gospel: Jesus' life, death, and resurrection as the only means of salvation.
- Your identity as a child of God, adopted and deeply loved.
- The authority of Scripture as God's revelation to mankind.
- The call to love God completely and love your neighbor as yourself.
- The presence and guidance of the Holy Spirit.
- The reality of the Kingdom, both now and not yet.
- The community of faith as the body of Christ.

> These don't shift. They're not up for negotiation. They're not context-dependent. They're true whether you feel them or not, whether they're convenient or not, whether your culture accepts them or not.

Fluid Practices - What Adapts

These are the specific ways you live out the fixed points in your current circumstances. They're the "how" that serves the "what." They should absolutely change as conditions change. Fluid practices include:

- The specific structure and timing of your prayer life.
- Which spiritual disciplines you emphasize in a given season.
- How you allocate your time, resources, and energy.
- The particular ministries or service opportunities you engage.
- Your approach to fasting, Sabbath, solitude, study, worship.
- The balance between engagement with and withdrawal from culture.
- The level of risk you take in obedience.
- How you navigate specific relational dynamics.
- The rhythm and intensity of your spiritual practices.

These *should* flex as tools, not fixed points. What works for one person might not work for you. What worked for you last year might not work this year. What serves you in one season might hinder you in another.

The mistake many Christians make is treating fluid practices as if they're fixed points. They find a spiritual rhythm that works—maybe a particular Bible reading plan, or a specific prayer practice, or a certain ministry involvement—and they lock it in. They make it a rule. They judge themselves and others by it.

Then circumstances change. The practice stops working. And instead of adapting the tool, they either force themselves to keep using it (which breeds resentment and spiritual exhaustion) or they abandon it entirely and feel like they've failed (which can breed guilt and disconnection).

> Neither response is navigation. Navigation means you adjust your practices to serve your ongoing connection to the fixed points.

The Core Tools

Here are the essential tools for navigating the discipleship journey. These aren't comprehensive and you'll discover others along the way, but these are foundational.

Tool 1: Regular Scripture Engagement

Notice I didn't say "Bible study" or "daily devotions" or any other specific method. I said regular Scripture engagement.

> *This is a fixed point: God's Word is truth and is essential for Christian growth. How you engage with scripture is a fluid practice.*

For some people, a structured reading plan for the Bible works beautifully. They need the framework, the progression, and the sense of completion. For others, that same plan feels like drudgery and kills engagement. Some people benefit from deep, slow reading of small scripture passages. Others thrive on reading larger sections to get the narrative flow. Some need to write as they read. Others need to pray through the text. Some do best first thing in the morning. Others find evening or midday more fruitful. The point isn't the method. The point is regular, engaged interaction with Scripture.

Often I read through the Bible in the course of a year, but not on a rigid schedule. I don't beat myself up if I miss days or fall behind. I read with a specific word, question or theme in mind for a period of time, often a year. For example, I read the entire Bible over a year with the lens of "contentment", asking God to show me what He wanted me to learn about finding security in Him. That time of focused reading changed me. Not because I followed a perfect plan, but because I engaged consistently with a specific openness to what God wanted to show me in that area of my wobble.

Application:

Don't adopt someone else's Bible reading method just because it worked for them. Experiment and try different approaches. Pay attention to what actually increases your engagement versus what feels like obligation. The standard isn't, "Am I following the plan correctly?" The standard is, "Am I actually engaging with God's Word? Is it shaping how I think and act?"

> If the answer is no, change your approach. The method of scripture reading is the tool. Scripture is the fixed point. Adjust the tool to

serve your connection to the fixed point.

Tool 2: Consistent Prayer Practice

Prayer is communication with God. That's the fixed point. How, when, and in what form you pray is fluid. For years, my prayer life was almost exclusively intercessory in the form of praying for other people, for situations, for needs outside myself. That's legitimate prayer, but it was also a way of avoiding personal responsibility for my own discipleship growth.

When I started taking responsibility for my discipleship, my prayers shifted. They became much more personal:

- "Father, how do I need to change my actions to align with Your will?"
- "Lord, what do You want me to learn from the mistakes I made today?"
- "Show me sins I've committed that I haven't repented of or that I'm not even aware of yet."
- "Are my attitudes today reflecting Christ?"

This type of prayer takes responsibility. It's not asking God to change my circumstances or fix other people. It's asking Him to change me, to show me what I'm responsible for, to guide my actions and attitudes. Different seasons require different prayer emphases.

- Sometimes you need to pray for others.
- Sometimes you need to pour out lament and complaint to God.
- Sometimes you need to sit in silence and simply be present with Him.
- Sometimes you need to pray through Scripture.
- Sometimes you need to pray while you're moving, such as walking, running, or working with your hands.

Application:

If your prayer life feels dead, change something. Try praying at a different time. Try praying out loud instead of silently, or vice versa. Try praying while you walk. Try praying Scripture back to God. Try keeping a written prayer journal. And most importantly, make your prayers about personal responsibility. Ask God to show you what you need to do, change, learn, or understand. Prayer should not be used for telling God what He needs to do, or what other people need to do.

> This shifts prayer from wishful thinking to actual navigation. Consistent communication with God through prayer is a powerful tool.

Tool 3: Authentic Community

We covered community as a principle. Now let's talk about it as a tool. Community isn't just showing up to church services or attending a weekly small group where you discuss a Bible study topic. That can be part of it, but it's not sufficient. Authentic community means you're in mutual, honest, regular relationship with other disciples who have permission to speak into your life and who you speak into in return. This requires intentionality. It doesn't just happen. You have to create space for it, structure for it, and commitment to it.

Here's what this has looked like in different seasons of my life. When my boys were young, my wife and I hosted consistent family meals around our dining room table. That table has been in eleven houses. It can't be taken apart, it's awkward to carry, it's extremely heavy, and my wife has wanted to replace it since day one. But it's been the site of nearly every pivotal conversation our family has had. We made it a no-distraction zone with no phones, no TV, just conversation. That was our community tool for that season.

Now that the boys are adults and living elsewhere, that same table serves a different function. We host small group gatherings and we have young singles and couples over for meals and robust conversation about life and faith. The tool of community and the purpose the table serves adapts to the season.

I've also led and been part of small groups that met weekly for years not for a semester or to just to study the Bible, but to actually do life together. To confess struggles, to celebrate victories, to pray specifically for each other's actual needs, to hold each other accountable for actual growth. Group discussions should have three parts each time you meet, fellowship, scriptural based discussion, and prayer. The fellowship section is greatly enhanced with occasional social gathering for food, laughter, and providing a safe place to just relate to one another. Our table has been central to fellowship within our small group as a safe place to just "be yourself".

Application:

Evaluate your community honestly. Do you have people in your life who know your actual Monday reality, not just your Sunday version? Do you have people who will ask you hard questions and speak truth to you? Do you have people you're in regular, consistent, mutual relationship with?

If not, you need to build a community. It might mean starting small—one person you meet with regularly for honest conversation. It might mean being the one to invite people into something deeper than surface-level interaction by inviting them to your home for a meal or getting involved in a small group in your church in order to build relationships.

Be intentional about building relationships. Once relationships are established, give a few select people permission to hold you accountable such as, "I need you to ask me about X. I need you to call me out when you see Y. I need you to check in on Z." You cannot rely solely on your local church to provide the community needed, you have to approach this intentionally.

Community as a tool requires structure and intentionality. Build it.

Tool 4: Rhythmic Self-Assessment

You can't navigate if you don't regularly assess your position. The harbor pilot is constantly checking instruments, visually scanning, communicating with others to verify location and heading. You need to do the same spiritually. This doesn't mean constant self-examination that breeds anxiety. It means regular, structured assessment that helps you recognize your patterns and make course corrections. I recommend three levels of assessment:

Daily: Actions and Attitudes Check - At the end of each day, ask yourself:

- What were my actions today? Did they reflect following Christ or serving

myself?
- What were my attitudes today? Did they reflect trust in God or anxiety about circumstances?
- Where did I take responsibility? Where did I avoid it?
- What do I need to repent of? What do I need to thank God for?
- This takes five minutes. It's not elaborate. It's just honest accounting.

Weekly: Pattern Recognition - Once a week, maybe Sunday evening or Monday morning, look at the pattern of the previous week:

- Where did I wobble this week? What tensions did I navigate?
- Did I wobble productively (course-correcting toward Christ) or destructively (drifting away)?
- What consistent struggles showed up? What consistent victories?
- Am I maintaining my core disciplines? Where am I slipping?

Quarterly: Trajectory Assessment - Every three months, do a more extensive review:

- Over the past three months, how has my wobble amplitude changed? Am I making smaller corrections more quickly, or am I swinging more wildly?
- What growth do I see? In what areas am I stagnated?
- Are my fluid practices still serving my connection to the fixed points, or do I need to adjust something?
- What's one specific area I need to focus on in the next quarter?

Application:
Build these assessments into your calendar. Literally schedule them. The daily check becomes a habit as a part of your evening routine. The weekly and quarterly assessments go on your calendar as appointments with yourself and God.

Don't skip them. These are your navigation instruments. Without regular self-assessment, you're guessing about your wobble position.

Tool 5: Focused Seasons of Emphasis

Here's a powerful tool I choose a specific area of focus for a defined season and orient my tools and practices around it. I mentioned earlier that I spent an entire year reading Scripture while asking God to teach me about contentment. Every day for a year, that was my question. And God answered it. Not in one dramatic moment, but through accumulated insights over time that fundamentally changed my sense of security in who I am in Christ.

This tool works because it harnesses the power of consistency (Principle 5) while maintaining preparation over prediction (Principle 4). You're not predicting exactly what God will do or teach you. Rather, you're preparing yourself to receive what He wants to give by maintaining a consistent focus. Other focused seasons I've had:

- A season focused on authenticity - specifically working to eliminate the gap between my public and private self.
- A season focused on my marriage - learning what it means to honor my wife above all others except my relationship with Christ.
- A season focused on contentment - which I've already mentioned.
- A season focused on listening - learning to recognize and respond to the Holy Spirit's promptings rather than always having my own agenda.

Each season lasts months, sometimes a year or more. Each has a specific focus that shaped my prayers, my Scripture reading, my conversations, and my self-assessment.

<u>Application:</u>

What area of your discipleship needs focused attention right now? Where are you wobbling most wildly? Where do you sense God prompting growth?

Choose one area. Not three. Not five. One. Then structure a season of focus. It could be three months, maybe six, maybe a year when you consistently orient your spiritual practices around that focus area. Read Scripture asking God to teach you about that area. Pray about it daily. Talk about it with your community. Assess yourself in that area. Keep a journal tracking insights and growth during the focus period.

> This isn't about perfecting that area. It's about giving sustained, focused attention to it and allowing God to work in you.

Tool 6: Physical Disciplines

This might surprise you, but physical practices are spiritual tools. I've been an athlete my whole life. I've trained for marathons, triathlons, and racquetball tournaments. I've learned that physical training teaches spiritual truths in ways that nothing else can. Consistency matters. One epic workout doesn't produce fitness but thirty solid workouts do. The same is true spiritually. Preparation beats prediction. I can't predict race day conditions such as weather, how my body will feel, what equipment issues might arise. But if I prepare consistently, I can handle whatever comes on race day. Your body tells the truth about your preparedness. You can't fake fitness or pretend your way through a marathon. Either you've done the work or you haven't. These lessons have direct spiritual application. And sometimes the physical practice itself becomes a spiritual practice.

Some of my most powerful prayers have occurred while running. The combination of physical exertion, mental focus, and time alone creates space for the Holy Spirit to work in ways that sitting still doesn't. Some of my biggest breakthroughs about surrender and trust have come through pushing my body to its limits and having to choose whether to quit or keep going, which is a direct parallel to discipleship challenges.

Application:

You don't have to become an athlete to use your body as a tool for spiritual formation. Maybe your walking while you pray. Maybe you fast in order for physical hunger to create spiritual hunger. Maybe you work with your hands on a project while meditating on Scripture. Maybe you push yourself physically in some way to learn about perseverance and dependence on God.

> Don't dismiss the physical practices from spiritual growth. Use the body God created for both physical and spiritual growth.

Tool 7: Boundaries as Freedom

This is one of the most counter intuitive tools, but it's essential to grasp. Boundaries create freedom. We tend to think boundaries are restrictions - things that limit us, confine us, keep us from doing what we want. But actually, boundaries are what enable freedom to flourish. I have some clear boundaries in my life, and those boundaries give me incredible freedom:

No alcohol. Ever. This boundary was established decades ago based on family history and personal conviction. Because it's a boundary and not a decision I make in the moment, I have complete freedom in social situations. I never have to decide. I never have to explain. I never have to navigate social pressure. The decision is made. That's freedom.

Never alone with another woman. This boundary protects my marriage and honors my wife. It has created some awkward moments as in waiting outside buildings rather than inside alone with a female, or in calling my son to be on speakerphone during a car ride when circumstances changed and I was alone in a car with a woman other than my wife. But the boundary gives me freedom and I don't have to navigate gray areas. I don't have to wonder if something is appropriate. The boundary is clear. That's freedom.

The family table as a no-distraction zone. When we're eating together, there are no phones, no TV, no distractions. Just conversation. This boundary created the space for the most important conversations our family has had. It was freedom from the tyranny of constant connectivity and gave us the freedom to actually be present with each other.

> *Boundaries work because they eliminate decision fatigue in areas where you've already decided what's wise. They protect you from your own*

rationalization in moments of weakness. They communicate your values clearly to others.

Application:
What boundaries do you need in your life?

- Maybe it's media boundaries - what you won't watch, what you won't consume, what you won't allow in your home.
- Maybe it's financial boundaries - what percentage you'll always give, what types of debt you won't take on, what financial decisions require spousal agreement.
- Maybe it's relational boundaries - who you won't be alone with, what conversations you won't engage in, what relationships you'll limit.
- Maybe it's time boundaries - what you won't schedule on certain days, what commitments you won't take on, what you'll protect.

Identify areas where you repeatedly struggle or where you want to ensure you never struggle. Establish clear boundaries. Communicate them to those around you. Honor them.

> The boundaries could feel restrictive at first. But, you'll discover that boundaries actually create freedom.

Building Your Sustainable Rhythm
You won't use all these tools all the time. That's not the point rather the point is to build a sustainable rhythm that serves your navigation in your current season. What's sustainable for a single person in their twenties is different from what's sustainable for a parent of young children. What works in a season of relative calm is different from what works in a season of crisis. What serves you when you're just beginning to follow Christ is different from what serves you after decades of discipleship. Your rhythm should include:

- Regular scripture engagement (in whatever form works for you now).

- Consistent prayer practice (adjusted to your current capacity).
- Authentic community (structured in a way that fits your life).
- Some form of self-assessment (to maintain awareness).
- At least one or two other tools that address your current growth areas.

That's it. That's enough. Don't try to do everything. Don't adopt someone else's entire system. Don't load yourself with obligations that aren't sustainable. Build a rhythm you can maintain. Then maintain it. Consistency over intensity, remember? And when your circumstances change such as when you enter a new season, or a crisis hits, as something shifts you give yourself permission to adjust the rhythm. The tools are meant to serve the navigation. If a tool stops serving, change it.

The Goal: Decreasing Amplitude

Remember the wobble factor? The goal isn't to eliminate the wobble. The goal is to decrease its amplitude over time. These tools help you do that. They help you recognize when you're wobbling. They help you make course corrections more quickly. They help you learn from your mistakes rather than just repeating them. They help you stay connected to your fixed points even when the conditions are chaotic.

Over months and years, as you consistently use these tools, you'll notice something: the wobble is still there, you're still navigating tensions, you're still making course corrections, but the corrections are smaller. You catch yourself drifting sooner. You recover faster. You don't swing as far off course before adjusting.

> That's maturity. Not the absence of wobble, but the reduction of its amplitude through consistent, faithful navigation. And that's what these tools are for.

> *Now, let's talk about what happens when you try to do this in the context of other people—because you can't navigate alone.*

8

Community in the Wobble

We need to expound upon Principle 6 about choosing community over independence more in depth. You cannot navigate your discipleship journey alone. I've said this before, but it bears repeating because it runs counter to how most of us actually live: discipleship is not a solo endeavor. The American church has absorbed a toxic individualism from the surrounding culture. We've made faith personal and private. We've reduced discipleship to "me and Jesus." We've turned spiritual growth into a self-improvement project that we pursue alone, in sprints, and maybe with occasional input from a pastor or a book.

That is not the picture of discipleship Jesus shows us in the Bible. Solo effort will not work if you want to actually grow. The wobble is difficult enough to navigate. You must have other people helping you see clearly, speaking truth, providing perspective, and walking alongside you.

Trying to navigate it alone is not just difficult, it's nearly impossible. You can't see your own blind spots. You can't recognize your own patterns while you're in them. You can't tell when you've crossed from productive wobble into destructive drift when you're the only one observing yourself. Your own internal dialogue will always be self-justifying, self-protective, and biased toward preserving your current trajectory.

You need external reference points (other people) to navigate effectively.

But not just any people, not casual church acquaintances, not surface-level friendships or performative small groups in which everyone maintains their Sunday morning personas. You need authentic community. You need fellow wobbling disciples who are willing to see you and be seen, who can help you navigate because they're navigating the same tensions themselves.

What Community Is Not

Before we talk about what authentic community looks like, let's clear away some common misconceptions.

Community is not accountability in the typical sense.

When most Christians hear "accountability," they think of someone checking up on them, asking if they did their quiet time, if they avoided certain sins, if they're keeping their commitments. It's framed as external monitoring to make sure you're doing what you're supposed to do.

That's not community. That's performance management.

Real community isn't about external monitoring. It's about mutual vulnerability and growth. It's not someone asking, "Are you doing what you're supposed to?" Rather, they ask, "Where are you actually struggling? What's really going on? How can we help each other grow?"

Community is not consuming together.

Many churches organize "community" around consumption such as watching a sermon together, discussing a study together, or attending an event together. You're in proximity with others and focused on the same content, but you're not actually in relationship. You can attend the same small group for years and never move beyond surface-level interaction. You can discuss theological concepts and biblical principles without ever revealing where you're actually wobbling in your own life.

That's not community. That's group consumption with a spiritual theme.

Community is not sameness.

We often gravitate toward people who are just like us, in the same life stage, similar background, struggles, theology, and style. We think community means finding "our people" who see everything the way we do. But that's not biblical community. The body of Christ is diverse by design. We all have different gifts, different perspectives, different backgrounds, different strengths and weaknesses. The whole point is that we need each other *because* we're different, not despite it.

> *If your community is just an echo chamber where everyone reinforces your existing views and no one challenges you, then it's not a community that helps you navigate. It may be a community that enables your drift.*

Community is not crisis response.

Some people only reach out to others when things fall apart. They isolate themselves when things are going well, then suddenly need community when they're in crisis. That's understandable and crisis does create urgency, but it's a backward viewpoint.

> *You need community before the crisis, so when the crisis comes, you already have people who know you, who can speak into your situation, and who can help you navigate. Community built in crisis is fragile. Community built over time is resilient.*

What Authentic Community Requires

So what does authentic community actually look like? What does it require from you?

Authenticity Over Performance

This is Principle 2 applied to relationships. You have to show up as your actual self, not your performed self. That means you tell the truth about where you are. Not where you wish you were. Not where you think you should be. Not where you were last year. Where you actually are right now. It may sound like:

- "I'm struggling with doubt, and it's scaring me."
- "My prayer life is non-existent, and I'm not sure I even care."
- "I keep falling into the same sin pattern, and I don't know how to break it."
- "My marriage is barely functioning, and I don't know what to do."
- "I'm angry at God, and I don't know if that's okay."

This level of honesty is terrifying for most people. Because we've been trained to perform. We've learned that admission of struggle is admission of failure. We've absorbed the message that mature Christians have it together.

> *Authenticity is the entry point for real community. If you won't show people your reality, they can't help you navigate it. They can only affirm your performance, which doesn't help you grow.*

Consistency Over Convenience

Authentic community requires commitment. You have to show up regularly, not just when it's convenient or when you feel like it. This is why I've emphasized rhythms and structures throughout this book. Community doesn't happen accidentally. It happens when you create space for it, protect that space, and show up consistently.

For years, our family protected dinner time at our table. No matter what else was happening, we ate together. That consistency created the foundation for the conversations that mattered. In different seasons, I've been part of small groups that met weekly for years. Not monthly. Not "when we can make it work." Weekly. Because consistency builds relationship with trust, and trust enables authenticity.

> *If you only connect with people sporadically, you'll never get past surface level. You'll spend all your time catching up on life logistics, and you'll never get to the stuff that really matters.*

Mutuality Over Hierarchy

Authentic community is not one person teaching or leading while everyone else receives. It's a mutual relationship. Everyone is both giving and receiving. Everyone is both speaking and listening. Everyone is both helping others navigate and being helped to navigate. This doesn't mean there's no role for more mature believers to mentor less mature ones. That's valuable and needed. But it should happen in the context of mutual relationship, not hierarchical transaction.

When I meet with younger couples now, they often ask me questions about life and faith based on the decades my wife and I have walked together. That's appropriate, but I'm also learning from them. They're seeing things I've stopped seeing and asking questions I've stopped asking. They're navigating challenges in a cultural moment in which I didn't navigate those same challenges.

> *We're all wobbling. We're all navigating our individual journeys. The goal is to help each other in our journeys.*

Specific Over Generic

"Pray for me" is generic. "Ask me every week if I've been honest with my wife about our finances" is specific.

"Keep me accountable" is generic. "Check in monthly about whether I'm still avoiding the conversation I need to have with my boss" is specific.

If you want community to actually help you navigate, you have to be specific about what you need. You have to give people permission to ask specific questions, to address particular areas, and to speak into your individual struggles. This requires you to know yourself well enough to identify what you actually need, and it's why the self-assessment tool from Chapter 7 is so important.

> *You can't ask for specific help if you don't know exactly where you're struggling.*

The Roles of Community in Navigation

Let's look at some specific ways community functions as a navigational tool.

Community Provides External Perspective

When you're wobbling, you often can't see it clearly. You're in the motion. You're experiencing the tensions. You're making decisions in real time with limited perspective. People close to you can see your pattern. They can notice when you're consistently wobbling in one direction. They can recognize when your course corrections are actually making things worse. They can spot the gap between what you say you value and what your actual choices reveal.

> *External perspective is invaluable. You don't have this perspective on yourself.*

I've had people in my life point out patterns I couldn't see. Some examples are "Every time you get stressed, you isolate and stop communicating." "You say you're trusting God, but your actions reveal you're trying to control everything." "You keep making the same choice and expecting different results." These observations weren't attacks, rather they were navigation assistance. They were helping me see what I couldn't see on my own.

Community Challenges Your Rationalization

Your internal dialogue is masterful at rationalization. You can justify almost anything to yourself if you work at it long enough. Have you thought:

- "This compromise is necessary given my circumstances."
- "Everyone struggles with this, so it's not that bad."

- "I'll address this later when things calm down."
- "This is just how I'm wired, and I can't change it."

Your own mind will find ways to make destructive drift look like reasonable navigation. Community challenges that. Other people can say: "I hear what you're saying, but I don't think that's actually true. Let's look at this more carefully."

> *Being challenged is rarely comfortable, but it's essential. Without it, you'll drift and convince yourself you're navigating.*

Community Encourages When You Want to Quit

The discipleship journey is long. There will be seasons when you're exhausted, discouraged, and ready to give up. When the wobble feels overwhelming. When you can't see any progress. When you wonder if any of this matters.

> *You need people who can remind you of truth. Who can point out growth you can't see. Who can encourage you to take the next step even when you don't feel like it.*

I've had seasons where I couldn't see any evidence of God's work in my life. Everything felt stale and stuck. And I had people who said. "I see it. Let me tell you what I've noticed..." And they would point out changes, growth, evidence of the Spirit's work that I couldn't see because I was too close to it. That encouragement kept me moving when I wanted to stop.

Community Celebrates Your Growth

When you experience breakthrough, when you make progress, when you see God work—you need people who will celebrate with you.

> *It isn't about pride or seeking affirmation. It's about joy being multiplied in community.*

When I finally broke through years of financial foolishness and paid off debt I never should have accumulated, I had people who celebrated that victory with me. Their joy multiplied mine. Their celebration confirmed that the hard work mattered. When I recognized and addressed patterns in my life that needed to change, I had people who noticed and affirmed that growth. Their recognition helped me see that the small steps were actually adding up to real change. Paul talks about rejoicing with those who rejoice. That's not just a nice sentiment. It's a function of community. Your victories are meant to be shared.

Different Levels of Community

Not all community relationships are the same. You'll have different levels with different people, and that's okay. In fact, it's necessary.

Level 1: The Broader Church Community

This is the congregation you're part of. You worship together, serve together and share the broader life of the church. These relationships might not be deeply personal, but they matter. You're part of the same church body. You're pursuing the same mission. You're oriented toward the same fixed points.

> *This level of community provides a sense of belonging, exposure to diversity within the body, opportunities to serve and be served, along with corporate worship and teaching.*

Level 2: Consistent Small Group

This is a smaller circle of maybe 6-12 people who meet regularly for deeper interaction. You're doing more than just attending church together. You're studying together, discussing together, praying together, serving together. These relationships are more personal. People know more about your life. You share more about your struggles. There's more mutual care and support.

> *This level of community provides consistent connection, opportunity for*

honest conversation, shared learning and growth, prayer support, and practical help in times of need.

Level 3: Close Discipleship Relationships

This is the innermost circle of maybe 2-4 people that have deep access to your life and you to theirs. These are the people who know your actual reality. They can ask you about anything in your life. You're in regular, honest, mutual relationship with. This might be a mentor relationship, a peer accountability partnership, or a small circle of close friends who are committed to each other's growth.

This level of community provides deep accountability, honest challenge, intimate knowledge of your patterns and struggles, specific prayer and support, and mutual encouragement in the hardest seasons.

You need all three levels of community, but Level 3 is where the real navigation help happens. This is where you can be most honest, most specific, most vulnerable. This is where people know you well enough to see your blind spots and love you enough to speak truth about them.

Building Your Community

To build your community, you should start with your local church. It is the first place to begin, but many churches don't have authentic discipleship groups. I've been in churches with and without this dynamic. I will never advocate going outside of the local church for building a small authentic discipleship group. Your most intimate group of people can be composed of people other than the ones in your church small group and can also contain believers from other churches. If you're reading this and realizing you don't have authentic community, especially at Level 3, here are some suggestions as to how to go about building it.

Start with Intentionality

Community doesn't happen by accident. You have to be intentional about creating it. That means you reach out. You invite. You initiate. You create the structure and rhythm that makes community possible. Maybe it's inviting someone to meet for coffee weekly. Maybe it's starting a small group in your home. Maybe it's asking a few people if they'd be willing to meet monthly for honest conversation and prayer about navigating your discipleship journeys.

Someone always has to initiate community. Let it be you.

Start Small
Don't try to build a community of twenty people all at once. Start with one or two. Find one person who seems to want something deeper than surface-level church friendship. Invite them to meet regularly. Be honest about what you're looking for and let people know, "I want to be in relationship with someone who's willing to be real about their struggles and help me be real about mine." Pray and ask God to highlight others to invite into community.

Start with one or two. Let it grow organically.

Be the First to Be Honest
Someone has to go first in being vulnerable, so let it be you. Don't wait for the other person to share something personal before you do. Don't test the waters with surface-level sharing to see if it's safe before you go deeper. Go first. Share something real. Model the authenticity you're looking for. Most people want deeper community but they're afraid to be the first one vulnerable.

By being vulnerable, you give others permission to do the same.

Give Specific Permission
As I've mentioned before, you need to tell people explicitly what you need from them.

- "I need you to ask me every week about my marriage. I need you to notice when I'm complaining about my wife and call me on it."
- "I need you to check in monthly about my prayer life. Not whether I'm doing a quiet time, but whether I'm actually engaging with God."
- "I need you to tell me when you see a gap between what I say I value and what my choices reveal."

> Don't expect people to magically know what you need. Tell them and be specific.

Commit to the Rhythm

Whatever structure you create—weekly coffee, monthly dinners, bi-weekly video calls—commit to it. Put it on your calendar. Protect that time. Show up even when it's inconvenient.

> Consistency builds trust. Trust enables depth. Depth enables real community.

Navigating Community Challenges

Community isn't easy. Even authentic, committed community will face challenges. Here are the common ones and suggestions as to how to navigate them.

Challenge 1: Someone Dominates

In any group, there's often one person who talks more, shares more, needs more. This can unbalance the community.

<u>Navigation:</u> Be direct but kind. "I value hearing from you, but I want to make sure we're hearing from everyone. Let's make space for others to share." Speak to the person privately, rather than in front of others. If you're the one dominating the conversation, recognize it and intentionally create space for

others to speak.

Challenge 2: Someone Performs

Even in intentional community, people sometimes default to performance rather than authenticity. They share the sanitized version of their life or us "church speak" regularly. They maintain the gap.

Navigation: Model deeper honesty. Ask specific follow-up questions that get past the surface. Create safety by being vulnerable yourself. Sometimes you might need to have a private conversation such as, "I value you, but I feel like we're staying at surface level. Can we try sharing specific instances and examples?"

Challenge 3: Someone Judges

When people share honestly, sometimes others respond with judgment rather than grace. This kills community.

Navigation: Address this immediately. "I don't think that response creates the safety we need. Let's remember we're all wobbling. We're here to help each other navigate, not judge." If someone consistently judges, they might not be ready for this level of community.

Challenge 4: Someone Ghosts

Sometimes people may stop showing up, stop responding, and start to drift away without explanation.

Navigation: Reach out directly. "I've missed you recently. Are you okay? Did something happen? How can we help?" Don't assume. Ask. Sometimes people pull away precisely when they need community most. Go after them.

Challenge 5: Life Circumstances Change

Occasionally someone in your close community moves. Someone's schedule shifts. The rhythm that worked stops working.

Navigation: Adapt. Community might look different in different seasons of life. Maybe you can move from weekly in-person to meetings via monthly video calls. Maybe you can add new people as others leave. The structure should be flexible. The commitment to connection is what matters.

Community and the Wobble

Here's what authentic community does for your navigation - it makes the wobble visible and manageable. When you're wobbling alone, you can't see the pattern. You just feel the motion. It may be disorienting and frightening.

When you're wobbling in community, others can see the pattern. Those in close community can tell you things like, "You're wobbling toward isolation again." Or "You're over-correcting toward rigidity." Or "I'm seeing growth—your wobble amplitude is decreasing." Community provides the external perspective that turns your wobble from chaotic motion into recognizable pattern. Once you can see the pattern, you can work to correct it.

Community also normalizes the wobble. When you see other people whom you respect, who are more mature in their faith wobbling too, it removes the shame. You realize that wobbling is normal, and this is how discipleship works. We're all navigating, course-correcting, learning and growing.

The question you should not be asking is, "Am I wobbling?" You are! The correct question is, "Am I wobbling with people who can help me navigate well? If you're wobbling alone, you're likely drifting and not recognizing it. If you're wobbling in community, you have the best chance of actually growing through the process and reducing amplitude of your wobble.

> You cannot navigate alone.

The tools equip you. The community supports you. But ultimately, you're the one doing the navigating. Let's talk about what that actually looks like in practice.

IV

Living the Wobble

9

Embracing the Tension

There's a lie we need to confront head-on. It's the lie that mature faith resolves all tension. We've been taught, either explicitly or implicitly that as you grow in your walk with Christ, things get clearer. The questions get answered and the tensions resolve. The wobble decreases until eventually you're sailing smoothly on a straight course toward the cross.

It's a comforting lie. It's also completely false.

Mature faith doesn't eliminate tension - it learns to navigate tension well. The three core tensions we identified - Conviction and Compromise, Certainty and Doubt, Zeal and Wisdom - don't disappear as you mature. If anything, they intensify. The more deeply you follow Christ, the more acutely you feel the pull of competing good choices and service, the more clearly you see the complexity of living faithfully in a broken world, the more you recognize how little you actually understand about God and His plans.

> The difference between immature faith and mature faith isn't the absence of tension, but how you navigate the tension.

Immature faith demands resolution and can't tolerate ambiguity. It forces every question into a binary answer. It collapses every tension into one pole or the other because it can't live in the middle. Mature faith embraces tension. It recognizes that some tensions aren't meant to be resolved but are meant to be navigated. It learns to live faithfully in the space between competing truths, holding both poles without collapsing either.

This chapter is about learning to do that. If you can't embrace tension, you'll spend your entire discipleship journey either swinging wildly from one extreme to the other or rigidly locking yourself into one position and calling it faithfulness. Neither is navigation. Both are forms of drift.

Why We Resist Tension

Before we talk about how to embrace tension, let's understand why we resist it so strongly.

We Equate Tension with Failure

Somewhere along the way, we absorbed the message that if we're experiencing tension in our walk with Christ, something is wrong. That good Christians shouldn't struggle with competing convictions. That mature believers should have their doubts resolved. That strong disciples should know exactly when to act and when to wait. Tension feels like evidence of inadequacy. Like we haven't studied enough, prayed enough, grown enough. We think if we were just more spiritual, the tension would disappear.

This is backwards thinking. Tension is often evidence of growth, not its absence. You feel tension precisely because you're taking both poles (negative and positive) seriously. You're not dismissing one in favor of the other. You're holding the fullness of the gospel, which is complex and multifaceted and refuses to be reduced to simple formulas.

We're Uncomfortable with Ambiguity

Our culture has trained us to want certainty, clarity, and quick resolution. We want answers, not questions. We want steps, not processes. We want to know and have concrete answers since ambiguity makes us anxious. Not knowing the right answer feels dangerous. Living in the tension of competing truths feels unstable.

But faith, by its very nature, involves ambiguity. "Now faith is the assurance of things hoped for, the conviction of things not seen" (Hebrews 11:1). Faith operates in the space where we don't have complete clarity, where we can't see the full picture, where we have to trust God even when we can't predict the outcome. Tension and ambiguity aren't obstacles to faith. They're the territory where faith operates.

We're Afraid of Being Wrong

If you embrace tension and say "I'm holding both conviction and flexibility, both certainty and doubt, both zeal and wisdom" you open yourself to criticism from every side. The people who've collapsed the tension toward conviction will accuse you of compromise. The people who've collapsed it toward flexibility will accuse you of rigidity. The certainty camp will call you doubting. The doubt camp will call you naive. The zeal faction will say you're cautious. The wisdom faction will say you're reckless.

It's much easier to pick a side and defend it. At least then you have clear allies and clear enemies. At least then you know you're "right" according to the standards of your chosen camp. But navigating tension means you're not trying to be right according to any camp's standards. You're trying to be faithful according to God's leading in your specific circumstances. That's harder and lonelier place to be, and it opens you to misunderstanding but it's also more honest.

Conviction and Compromise - Holding the Line While Crossing It

You have convictions or beliefs about how you should live as a disciple of Christ, what you should prioritize, and how you should steward your resources and relationships. These convictions come from Scripture, from the Holy Spirit's work in you, and from your understanding of what it means to follow Jesus faithfully.

But you also live in the world. You have responsibilities and limitations. You have relationships with people who don't share your convictions, and you encounter situations where your ideals clash with your realities. *The immature response is to collapse this tension in one of two directions:*

Collapsing toward conviction says: "I will never compromise. I will hold the line no matter the cost. My convictions are absolute and non-negotiable in every circumstance." This sounds spiritual. It sounds like faithfulness. But it often becomes rigidity. It can't adapt to complex circumstances. It judges everyone who doesn't share its specific convictions. It confuses cultural preferences with biblical mandates. It becomes Pharisaical majoring in minors, straining gnats while swallowing camels.

Collapsing toward compromise says: "I need to be realistic. My convictions are ideals, but life is complicated. I have to be flexible, accommodating, and practical. I can't expect to live out my convictions perfectly given my circumstances." This sounds humble, and like grace. But it often becomes rationalization. It loses its distinctiveness and becomes indistinguishable from the surrounding culture. It calls compromise wisdom and accommodation love, when really it's just avoiding the cost of conviction.

> *Neither extreme is faithful navigation. Both are forms of drift that avoid the tension by choosing one side over the other.*

Mature navigation holds the tension

Maturing disciples say "I have deep convictions about how I should live, and I'm going to pursue them seriously, even when it's costly. But I also recognize that I live in a complex world where my convictions sometimes clash with competing choices, where absolute consistency might require sacrificing other values I also hold, and where faithfulness might look different in varying circumstances."

In this scenario you're constantly navigating. Constantly assessing. Constantly asking, "Where do I hold the line? Where do I adapt? What's actually at stake here? Is this a hill to die on or a place to extend grace?"

Here's n real world example of how to hold tension. I have a conviction about simplicity and generosity. I believe followers of Jesus should live with open hands, trusting God's provision rather than accumulating security. That conviction comes from Scripture and from the Spirit's work in me. But I also have responsibilities. I have a wife whose sense of security is different from mine. I have aging parents who might need care. I live in an economy where certain forms of saving and planning are wise stewardship, not lack of faith.

I could collapse this tension toward conviction by saying: "We're going to give everything away and live radically, trusting God for daily provision." That might sound spiritual, but it would violate my responsibility to my wife and potentially to my parents.

Or I could collapse it toward compromise by saying: "Well, we live in the real world. We need to save for retirement and build security. Radical generosity isn't realistic for our circumstances." That might sound practical, but it would rationalize away the conviction God has given me.

Instead, I navigate the tension. We give significantly more than is "wise" by conventional standards. But we also maintain some savings for legitimate needs. We regularly revisit our financial decisions, asking: "Are we holding our resources with open hands? Are we trusting God or trusting our bank account? Where do we need to push more toward generosity? Where is wisdom actually calling for different choices?" It's a constant navigation. Sometimes I lean more toward conviction by giving in ways that feel risky and uncomfortable. Sometimes I lean more toward wisdom by making choices that feel like compromise but that I believe are actually responsible.

> The point isn't that I've found the perfect balance. The point is that I'm holding the tension. I'm not collapsing it. I'm not resolving it by choosing one pole and dismissing the other. That's what embracing this tension like. You can navigate tension successfully by listening to and obeying the guidance of the Holy Spirit.

Application:
Where do you feel the pull between conviction and compromise in your own life?

- Maybe it's how you spend your time - convicted about Sabbath and rest, but facing real demands that seem to require constant availability.
- Maybe it's how you engage culture - convicted about holiness and separation, but also called to love and engage your neighbors who live differently.
- Maybe it's how you handle conflict - convicted about truth-telling and confrontation, but also aware of timing and relationship dynamics.
- Don't resolve the tension by choosing a side. Hold it. Navigate it. Ask God how to navigate it faithfully in the present circumstances and with your current relationships.

The answer He provides might be different next year. It might even be different next month. That's okay. You're navigating, not locking into a permanent position.

Certainty and Doubt - Believing While Questioning

Many of us want to be certain. About God's existence, His character, His promises, and His will for your life. Certainty feels like faith. Doubt feels like its opposite. What happens when you encounter mystery and suffering that doesn't make sense? What about prayers that go unanswered and Biblical passages that seem contradictory? Or theological questions without tidy answers and life experiences that shake what you thought you knew?

Or maybe your doubt is less intellectual and more visceral. You wake up one day and the faith that felt solid yesterday feels hollow today. You pray and sense nothing. You read Scripture and they're just words on a page. You look at your life and can't see God's hand anywhere. *Again, the immature response is to collapse the tension:*

Collapsing toward certainty says: "I believe. I will not doubt. If I'm experiencing doubt, I will push it down, ignore it, and rebuke it. I will speak with confidence even when I don't feel confident. I will double down on what I know to be true." This can create a brittle faith. It's faith that can't acknowledge questions, a faith that treats doubt as sin rather than as a normal part of the journey, and a faith that becomes defensive and rigid because it can't tolerate vulnerability.

Collapsing toward doubt says: "I can't know anything for certain. All my beliefs are provisional. I'll hold everything loosely. I won't commit to anything I can't prove. Humility means perpetual uncertainty." This can create an untethered faith. A faith that has no anchor. A faith that can't make commitments or take stands. A faith that uses doubt as a shield against obedience - "I can't act because I'm not certain."

Mature navigation holds the tension

Maturing disciples understand that, while truth is held firmly, there are some questions that can't be answered and some mystery that can't be explained. My belief doesn't require the absence of doubt. My doubt doesn't negate the reality of my faith. This is actually the biblical pattern. Here are some examples:

- Think about the father who brought his demon-possessed son to Jesus saying: "I believe; help my unbelief!" (Mark 9:24). Both in the same breath. Not one or the other. Both.
- Thomas, who declared he wouldn't believe unless he saw and touched Jesus' wounds but then, when he did see, made the most profound confession in the Gospels: "My Lord and my God!" His doubt didn't disqualify him. It led him to deeper faith.
- Job, who questioned God relentlessly, who accused God of injustice, who demanded answers and who God ultimately commended for speaking rightly about Him, while condemning the friends who maintained rigid theological certainty.
- The Psalms, which are full of both confidence and complaint, both trust and questioning, often in the same psalm, sometimes in the same verse.

> The Bible doesn't resolve the tension between certainty and doubt. It models holding it.

I've had seasons of profound certainty. There have been times when God's presence was palpable, when Scripture came alive, when prayer felt like conversation, and when I could see His hand clearly at work. And I've had seasons of profound doubt. Like times when God felt absent, when Scripture felt dead, when prayer felt like talking to the ceiling, when nothing made sense.

The mature response isn't to pretend the doubt away during the hard seasons or to dismiss the certainty as emotion during the clear seasons. The mature response is to hold both as part of the journey. During seasons of certainty, it's easier to say, "This is a gift. I receive it. But I know seasons change, and I'm building on the foundation of what I know to be true, not on the feeling of certainty." During seasons of doubt it's difficult to say, "This is hard. I acknowledge it. But I'm going to continue acting on what I know to be true from seasons of certainty, even though I don't feel it right now."

I keep showing up. I keep engaging. I keep taking the next faithful step. Not because I've resolved the tension between certainty and doubt, but because I'm holding it.

Application:

Give yourself permission to doubt without abandoning faith. If you're in a season of certainty, don't judge people who are in a season of doubt. Remember that seasons change and we need to build foundations that will hold when the feelings shift.

If you're in a season of doubt, don't judge yourself for not having certainty. Don't pretend feelings you don't have. But also don't let the doubt become an excuse for disengagement. Keep showing up. Keep acting on what you knew to be true in clearer seasons. And most importantly, be honest about where you are. With yourself, with God, and with your community. Don't perform certainty you don't feel. Don't weaponize doubt against yourself or others.

Hold the tension certainty and doubt. Both belief and doubt can coexist in a faithful heart.

Zeal and Wisdom - Moving Boldly While Counting the Cost

When you encounter truth, when the Spirit stirs you, when you see clearly what God is calling you to and you feel zeal - Urgent, passionate, ready-to-act-now zeal. You want to respond immediately - You want to reorganize your life around this truth right now. But you also have experience. You've seen what happens when people act on pure zeal without wisdom. You've watched people burn out, burn others, make commitments they can't keep, and create wreckage in their wake. You know the cost of unchecked passion. *Once again, the immature response is to collapse the tension:*

Collapsing toward zeal: "God has spoken. I will obey immediately and completely. I will act boldly without hesitation. Caution is fear. Analysis is paralysis. I will move." This can create chaos. It can lead to impulsive decisions that weren't actually God's leading but we're just your own passion. It can burn relationships, destroy trust, and create instability. It can mistake intensity for faithfulness.

Collapsing toward wisdom: "I need to think this through. I need to consider all the implications. I need to seek counsel and wait for confirmation to make sure the timing is right. I won't act until I'm certain." This can create paralysis. It can turn wisdom into an excuse for disobedience. It can rationalize away costly obedience by calling it unwise. It can mistake caution for faithfulness.

> *Again, neither extreme is faithful navigation. Both are forms of drift that avoids the tension by choosing on side over the other.*

Mature navigation holds the tension

Maturing disciples say, "I feel the pull of this conviction strongly, and I'm going to take it seriously. But I'm also going to test it, seek counsel, consider the implications, and move thoughtfully rather than impulsively."

This doesn't mean you never move quickly. Sometimes the Spirit prompts immediate action, and wisdom is recognizing that and responding appropriately. But even then, you're holding both as you move with urgency and are aware of what you're doing and why.

I've felt this tension repeatedly in my life. Major decisions such as job changes, ministry opportunities, and financial commitments when I felt strong conviction but also had to count the cost. When we joined a church plant that moved from Illinois to Texas - selling our house, leaving jobs, giving financially, uprooting our lives - it was a decision that required both zeal and wisdom. The zeal said, "This is what God is calling us to. We're going." The wisdom said, "Let's make sure we're hearing this clearly. Let's involve our family in the decision. Let's count the actual costs and make sure we're prepared." We held both. We moved with conviction, but not recklessly. We took a leap of faith, but not a blind one.

Other times, I've felt strong conviction about something and the wisdom side of the equation said, "Not yet. The timing isn't right. You need to prepare more. You need to build more foundation first." And I've had to hold the tension of feeling urgently called while wisely waiting.

> The key is not to dismiss zeal as just emotion and ignore it, nor use wisdom as an excuse to delay obedience but to allow both to inform decision and obedience.

Application:

When you feel strong conviction about something or a call to action, a needed change, or a new direction, don't immediately act and don't immediately dismiss. Instead, hold the tension. Ask yourself:

- Is this conviction from God or from my own desire?
- What's the cost of acting on this? Can I actually sustain that cost?
- What's the cost of not acting on this? What am I risking by waiting?
- What does wisdom say about timing and approach?

- What does zeal say about urgency and importance?
- How do I honor both without collapsing into either?

Sometimes you'll lean more toward zeal and take risks, you'll move before you're comfortable, and you'll trust God with uncertain outcomes. Sometimes you'll lean more toward wisdom and you'll wait, you'll prepare, and you'll count costs before committing. Both are faithful responses.

The key to navigate, not collapse. Learn to hold the tension.

The Practice of Holding Tension

So how do you hold tension without collapsing it?

Name the Tension

First, recognize and name the specific tension you're navigating. Don't just feel the discomfort—identify its source.

- "I'm feeling the tension between my conviction about X and the reality of Y."
- "I'm experiencing both certainty about God's character and doubt about His presence in this situation."
- "I sense both urgency to act and wisdom counseling caution."

Naming it gives you something to work with rather than just emotional confusion.

Resist the Demand for Resolution

When you feel the pull of tension, your instinct will be to resolve it—to pick a side, to find the answer, to eliminate the discomfort. Resist that instinct. Say to yourself, "Tension is okay. I don't need to resolve it right now. I can hold both poles and navigate between them." It takes practice. We're so conditioned to want resolution that learning to be comfortable in tension is a skill must be developed.

Seek Perspective

This is where community is essential. Other people can help you see when you're collapsing a tension you should be holding.

- "I hear you talking about your conviction, but I'm not hearing any acknowledgment of the practical constraints. Can we talk about both?"
- "You're expressing a lot of doubt, but I know there are things you're certain about. Can you speak those too?"
- "You sound like you're ready to act immediately. What does wisdom say about this decision?"

Community helps you maintain both poles when your own tendency is to collapse toward one.

Navigate Practically

Even while holding tension, you still have to make decisions and take action. So ask yourself, "Given that I'm holding both poles of this tension, what's the next faithful step?"

You might not be able to resolve the tension, but you can make a decision that honors both sides. You can take action that moves you forward while remaining open to course correction.

Revisit Regularly

Tensions aren't one-time decisions. They're ongoing navigation, so revisit them regularly.

- "Am I still holding this tension, or have I collapsed toward one pole?"
- "Do I need to adjust my course? Am I leaning too far in one direction?"
- "Has the situation changed in ways that shift how I navigate this tension?"

Regular reassessment keeps you actively navigating rather than passively drifting.

The Gift of Tension

The tension isn't punishment, evidence of failure, or a problem to be solved.

> *The tension is the territory of maturing faith.*

It's where you learn to trust God when you can't see Him clearly. It's where you develop wisdom through practice. It's where you discover that faithfulness isn't about having all the answers. It's about following Jesus even when the path is complex. The wobble happens in the tension. The course corrections happen because you're navigating competing choices, holding multiple truths, and responding to dynamic conditions.

If faith were simple, if every decision were obvious, if every tension resolved cleanly, if the path were straight, you wouldn't need faith. You'd just need a map. But God hasn't given you a map with every turn marked. He's given you a compass that points to Jesus, principles that orient you, tools to navigate, community to support you, and the Holy Spirit to guide you. And He's placed you in a world that's complex, broken, and beautiful. Where faithfulness requires wisdom. Where love requires discernment. Where conviction requires humility.

The tension is where you learn to follow Him well. So don't fight the tension. Don't collapse it. Don't resolve it prematurely. Embrace it. Navigate it. Let it form you.

> The wobble isn't a bug - it's a common feature. And learning to hold tension is learning to navigate faithfully in whatever conditions God has you sailing.

> *You've learned to recognize your pattern. You've built your tools. You've*

engaged your community. You've learned to hold tension. Now let's talk about what this looks like over the long haul – because this isn't a sprint. It's a marathon that lasts your entire Christian life.

10

The Long View

If you've made it this far in the book, you understand the wobble. You recognize your patterns. You've identified your fixed points and your fluid practices. You have tools and community. You're learning to hold tension without collapsing it.

But here's a question that disturbs most disciples at some point in their journey – Is any of this actually working? You look at your life and you still see the same struggles. You still fall into familiar patterns. You still make the same mistakes. You still wobble, sometimes wildly. You wonder "Am I actually growing? Am I making any progress? Or am I just spinning in circles, convincing myself I'm navigating when I'm really just drifting?" This is where the long view becomes essential.

> *Growth in discipleship is almost always invisible in the short term and unmistakable in the long term.*

Day to day, you can't see it and week to week, you might catch glimpses and month to month, you're not sure. But year to year, decade to decade is often when you look back on your discipleship journey with honest eyes the evidence of the Spirit's work is undeniable.

The problem is, we don't naturally take the long view. We're conditioned for immediate results. We want to see progress now and desire measurable gains quickly. We want to know that our effort is producing results. But discipleship doesn't work that way. It's not a sprint. It's a marathon. It's a lifetime journey of continual formation into Christ likeness that won't be complete until you see Christ face to face.

> *If you don't learn to take the long view, you'll get discouraged. You'll convince yourself that nothing is changing and that the wobble isn't worth navigating.*

This chapter is about learning to measure your growth accurately. It's about recognizing the evidence of the Holy Spirit's work even when it's not dramatic. It's about maintaining faithfulness over decades, not just days, and embracing the reality that, this side of heaven, you will always be wobbling. And that's exactly as it should be.

Why the Wobble Is Evidence of the Holy Spirit's Work

Let's start with a reframe that is essential for the long view. The fact is that the wobble itself is evidence that the Spirit is working in you. Not the absence of wobble. Not the achievement of a straight line. The presence of active, engaged, responsive navigation is evidence. Following are some thoughts as to why.

The Wobble Means You're Moving

Dead things don't wobble. Stagnant things don't correct course and static things don't respond to changing conditions. If your faith looks exactly the same today as it did five years ago with the same beliefs, same practices, same understanding, same struggles, and same victories, that's not stability. That's stagnation.

> *The wobble indicates that something is happening in your faith journey. You're engaging with God. You're responding to the Spirit. You're learning, adjusting and growing. You're faith is alive.*

The Wobble Means You're Taking Both Poles of Tension Seriously

If you never felt the tension between conviction and compromise, it would mean you've collapsed entirely toward one pole. You've either become so rigid that you can't adapt to real circumstances, or so accommodating that you've lost your distinctiveness.

If you never felt the tension between certainty and doubt, it would mean you've either achieved a false certainty that can't acknowledge mystery, or you've settled into a perpetual uncertainty that can't make commitments.

> *The wobble indicates you're holding the fullness of the gospel. You're not reducing it to simple answers. You're living in the complexity of following a God who is both transcendent and imminent, both sovereign and intimate, both just and merciful.*

The Wobble Means You're Responsive

A ship on an older style autopilot follows a programmed course regardless of conditions. It doesn't wobble, rather it just plows ahead according to the preset plan. If the conditions change, the autopilot doesn't adjust. It just keeps going in the wrong direction. New autopilots use GPS to adjust and correct direction. The wobble means you're not on an old style autopilot and you're paying attention. You're responding to the Holy Spirit's prompting and adjusting based on what you're learning along your journey. You're actively navigating, not just following a predetermined script.

> *This is what it means to be led by the Spirit. There is not a straight-line path or predetermined script, but rather we respond to His leading as we go. When you look at your life and see the wobble, don't interpret it as failure. Recognize it as evidence that the Holy Spirit is actively guiding you.*

Measuring Progress in a Non-Linear Journey

If growth isn't a straight line, how do you measure it? How do you know if you're actually progressing or just moving in circles?

> The measure of spiritual growth is a reduction in the *amplitude* of the wobble, not its *presence*.

Remember the mental image from earlier in the book of the path toward the cross with the wobble on either side of the path. You're never going to eliminate the wobble, but over time, as you mature, the amplitude should decrease and the swings should be smaller. The course corrections should be quicker and less dramatic.

What Decreasing Amplitude Looks Like
  You recognize drift sooner. In early discipleship, you might drift for months before realizing you're off course. As you mature, you catch it in weeks, then days, then sometimes hours. You've developed sensitivity to the Spirit's promptings and awareness of your own patterns.
  You recover faster. When you do drift or make a mistake, you don't stay in it as long. You repent more quickly. You course-correct more readily. You don't wallow in guilt or justify your position. You acknowledge, adjust, and move forward.
  You repeat mistakes less frequently. You'll never stop making mistakes entirely. But the same mistake that used to derail you for months, now happens less often. And when it does happen, you know how to navigate it because you've learned from previous iterations.
  You need less external correction. In early discipleship, you often need other people to point out when you're off course. As you mature, you internalize that perspective. You start catching yourself. You still need community, but you're more self-aware.
  You maintain stability in chaos. When circumstances get difficult, you

don't swing as wildly. You have foundations that hold. You have practices that sustain you. You wobble, but you don't capsize.

You extend more grace to others. As you become more aware of your own wobble and God's patience with you, you become more patient with others who are wobbling. You stop judging their journey by the standard of a straight line you now know doesn't exist.

These are the signs of decreasing amplitude and are how you measure growth over the long haul.

Looking Back to See Forward

The most powerful tool for taking the long view is intentional reflection on your past. I can look back over decades of following Christ and see patterns I couldn't see at the time. I can see how God was working in seasons when I thought He was absent. I can see growth that was invisible in the moment but undeniable in retrospect.

My Financial Wobble

In my early twenties, I inherited a significant amount of money and quickly squandered it. I made foolish decision after foolish decision. I accumulated debt and was advised to file bankruptcy. At the time, it felt like total failure. Like I'd ruined my financial future and proven I couldn't be trusted with resources. But looking back with the long view, I can see what God was doing. That season taught me:

- The difference between a need and a want.
- The cost of living above my means to maintain an image.
- The discipline of paying off debt honoring my commitments rather than taking an easy way out.
- The freedom that comes from tithing, even at my lowest income level, and giving God first place rather than trying to control everything myself.
- The foundation for how I would eventually teach my sons about money,

responsibility, and stewardship.

Was it a wobble? Absolutely. A massive one. But it wasn't wasted. God used it. The amplitude of my financial wobble has decreased dramatically since then—not because I've perfected financial management, but because I learned through that season.

My Identity Wobble

For years, I found my identity in my roles as a military officer, weather forecaster, athlete, pastor, and father. Each role became the lens through which I understood myself. When roles changed or ended, I experienced identity crisis. At the time, each transition felt destabilizing. Like I was losing myself and I didn't know who I was anymore.

But looking back, I can see God was teaching me that my identity is in Christ alone. Not in what I do. Not in the roles I play. Not in the titles I hold or the accomplishments I achieve. It took decades for this lesson to settle deep within me. I'm still learning it. But the amplitude of my identity wobble has decreased. I can navigate role changes now without the same level of existential crisis because I know who I am in Christ, regardless of what role I'm currently playing.

My Contentment Wobble

I spent much of my adult life looking for the next thing, the next promotion, the next race, the next opportunity. I was never fully present because I was always scanning the horizon for what was coming. At the time, I told myself this was ambition, drive, and vision. But actually, it was discontentment and restlessness. An inability to receive the present moment as a gift.

It wasn't until I spent an entire year reading Scripture with the specific lens of contentment by asking God every day to teach me what it means to be secure in Him that this began to shift. Looking back, I can see how that one focused season changed the trajectory of my discipleship. The amplitude of my contentment wobble has decreased. I still feel the pull to look ahead, but I catch it sooner. I can be present more consistently. I can receive today as

God's gift rather than always wishing for tomorrow.

These are just a few examples. I could give dozens more. The point is - I can only see my growth by looking back over years and decades. In the moment, each wobble felt like failure. In retrospect, each wobble was an opportunity for growth.

Application:

Look back over the past five years of your life. Ask yourself:

- What struggles am I still navigating? (Don't judge this—name it.)
- How has my response to those struggles changed?
- What lessons have I learned that I didn't know five years ago?
- Where do I see evidence of decreasing amplitude?
- What wobbles have actually been formative, even though they felt like failure?

Write it down. Be specific. Because you need evidence to combat the lie that nothing is changing. Then do the same exercise looking back ten years. Try twenty years if you can. You'll see patterns you can't see looking at your life day to day. You'll see growth that's invisible in the short term but unmistakable in the long term.

Why You'll Never "Arrive"

There is a hard truth that you need to embrace for the long view. There is no point in your discipleship journey this side of heaven where you've "made it." Where the wobble stops and you no longer need to navigate. Where you're a fully mature Christian and can coast. Even in my sixth decade of life, I'm still wobbling. Still making course corrections. Still learning things about myself that need to change. Still being surprised by areas of immaturity I didn't know were there.

Paul, at the end of his life and ministry, wrote: "Not that I have already obtained this or am already perfect, but I press on to make it my own, because

Christ Jesus has made me his own" (Philippians 3:12). Yes, Paul. The apostle who wrote most of the New Testament. Who planted churches across the known world. Who had profound theological insight and powerful spiritual experiences. The one who gave his life to the spread of the gospel. And he still said: "Not that I have already obtained this."

If Paul didn't arrive, neither will you.

That's not a disappointing statement, it's actually freeing. It means you can stop judging yourself by the vague standard of "arrival". You can stop comparing yourself to some imaginary version of a "mature Christian" who has it all together. You can stop beating yourself up for still struggling with issues you thought you'd overcome years ago. You're in process. You will always be in process. Until you see Christ face to face, the work of formation continues.

This is normal. This is expected. This is the journey.

The Freedom of Accepting the Process

When you truly accept that you'll never arrive and you stop orienting your discipleship toward some future state of perfection, something beautiful happens. You become free to actually engage the present.

- Instead of constantly measuring yourself against where you think you should be, you can honestly assess where you actually are and take the next faithful step in your discipleship journey from that position.
- Instead of hiding your struggles because they're evidence you haven't "arrived," you can be honest about them because you've accepted that struggling is part of the journey.
- Instead of performing maturity you don't have, you can be authentic about your actual growth and your actual limitations.

- Instead of being paralyzed by the gap between your ideal and your reality, you can make progress from your reality toward your ideal in knowing the ideal will always be ahead of you, and that's okay.

Paul modeled this. In the same passage where he said he hadn't obtained perfection, he also said: "One thing I do: forgetting what lies behind and straining forward to what lies ahead, I press on toward the goal for the prize of the upward call of God in Christ Jesus" (Philippians 3:13-14). Paul recognized that his life was in God's hands and pressed on.

He let go of what was behind—the failures and the successes both. He didn't dwell on past mistakes or rest on past victories. He focused forward. He strained toward what lay ahead—not perfectly, not without wobbling, but with consistent orientation toward Christ.

> That's the long view. That's sustainable discipleship. That's how you navigate faithfully over decades.

Maintaining Faithfulness Over Time

So how do you maintain faithfulness to Jesus over the long haul? How do you keep going when the journey is measured in decades, not days?

Remember Your Why - Why are you following Christ? Not just theologically, "Because He saved me", although that's true. But practically, personally, in your specific life: why?

For me, it's because I've seen too much evidence of the Holy Spirit's work in my life to walk away. I've experienced too many moments where God showed up in ways I couldn't manufacture. I've been carried through seasons I couldn't navigate alone. I've been changed in ways I couldn't change myself. I follow Christ because no other framework for life made sense once I encountered Him.

When discipleship gets hard, and it will, you need to remember why you're on this journey. Not as an obligation. Not as a performance. But as a response to a God who has revealed Himself to you and continues to work in you.

Celebrate the Small Wins – Growth in discipleship is usually incremental. Small steps repeated over time. Minor course corrections that add up. If you only celebrate the dramatic breakthroughs, you'll miss most of the growth. Learn to notice and celebrate the small wins, such as:

- You recognized you were drifting and corrected course before it became a crisis.
- You had a difficult conversation you would have avoided in the past.
- You extended grace in a situation where previously you would have judged.
- You practiced a spiritual discipline consistently for a month, and then a year.
- You asked for help instead of isolating yourself.

These may not seem dramatic, but they're growth. And they deserve acknowledgment.

Adjust Your Practices as Needed – What worked in one season of life won't necessarily work in the next. Your rhythm at 25 as a single person won't work at 35 with young children. Your practices during a season of relative stability won't work during a season of crisis. Don't lock yourself into methods. Remain flexible with your tools while staying oriented toward your fixed points.

I've adjusted my spiritual practices dozens of times over the decades. Different Bible reading approaches. Different prayer rhythms. Different forms of community. Different ways of serving. The fluidity doesn't indicate instability. It indicates responsive navigation.

Stay Connected to Community – You cannot maintain faithfulness over decades alone. You need people who knew you ten years ago and can remind you how you've grown. You need people who are ahead of you in the journey and can encourage you that the wobble continues but the amplitude decreases. You need people who are behind you in the journey and give you perspective on how far you've come.

Community provides continuity. It provides perspective. It provides correction and encouragement and celebration. The seasons when I've been most isolated are the seasons when I've drifted most. The seasons when I've been most connected are the seasons when I've navigated most faithfully.

Give Yourself Grace - This is perhaps the most important practice for the long haul: extend to yourself the grace that God extends to you. You will wobble, you will make mistakes, you will fail, you will drift, you will repeat patterns you thought you'd broken and you will disappoint yourself.

Grace doesn't mean you excuse these things or dismiss them. It means you acknowledge them, repent where needed, learn from mistakes, and keep moving forward. Self-condemnation doesn't produce growth. It produces either paralysis or performance. Grace produces actual transformation. God is patient with your process, so you need to be patient with it too.

The Goal is Faithfulness, Not Perfection

As you take the long view, let's clarify what you're actually aiming for. It's not perfection or arrival and not the elimination of wobble. It's faithfulness in your discipleship journey.

- Faithfulness means you keep showing up. You keep engaging. You keep taking the next step even when you can't see the full path.
- Faithfulness means you keep listening for the Holy Spirit's voice and responding when you hear it, even if your response is imperfect.
- Faithfulness means you stay oriented toward Christ even when you're wobbling wildly.
- Faithfulness means you take responsibility for your actions and attitudes rather than blaming circumstances or others.
- Faithfulness means you remain in community even when it's difficult.
- Faithfulness means you hold the tension without collapsing it.
- Faithfulness means you navigate with honesty rather than perform with pretense.

God is not seeking perfection. He seeks your faithfulness. He will say, "Well done, good and faithful servant." Not "perfect servant." Faithful.

The Evidence You're Looking For

So when you look back over your discipleship journey and ask, "Is any of this working?"—here's the evidence you should be looking for:

- Are you more like Christ than you were five years ago? Ten years ago? Be honest. Are you more loving, more patient, more humble, more generous, more honest, more courageous?
- Are you more aware of your sin and more quick to repent? You'll never be sinless this side of heaven, but are you more aware of your sin and more responsive?
- Are you more dependent on God and less confident in yourself? Do you trust Him more? Turn to Him more quickly?
- Are you more authentic and less performative? Is the gap between your public and private self narrowing?
- Are you more engaged with Scripture and prayer, even if your methods have changed?
- Are you more connected in genuine community?
- Are you more able to hold tension without collapsing it?
- Is the amplitude of your wobble decreasing, even though the wobble itself continues?

If you can answer yes to most of these questions, the Holy Spirit is working in you. You're growing. The navigation is producing fruit. It might not be dramatic. It might not be what you expected. But it's real. And that's what the long view reveals.

Looking Forward

I don't know how many days I have left on the earth, but God knows. What I do know is this - I will be wobbling in my discipleship until the day I die. I will be navigating until I reach the shore. I will be in process until I see Christ face to face. And I'm okay with that. I'm actually grateful for it. Because the wobble means I'm alive. It means I'm engaging. It means I haven't settled into stagnation or rigidity or comfortable drift. It means the Spirit is still working, still forming, still leading.

When I look back over the decades I've already lived, I can see His faithfulness. I can see growth I couldn't see in the moment. I can see how He's used every wobble, every mistake, and every course correction to form me more into the image of Christ.

Not perfectly. Not completely. But unmistakably.

That's the evidence you need when you wonder if any of this is working. Take the long view and look back at your life with honesty. See the evidence of the Holy Spirit's work. Celebrate the decreasing amplitude even while accepting the continuing wobble, and then press on faithfully. One wobbling step at a time for as long as God gives you breath.

> The journey isn't about arriving. It's about following. And following means you keep moving, keep adjusting, keep navigating all the way home.

You've learned the principles, built the tools, engaged community, embraced tension, and taken the long view. Now there's only one question left: What will you do with what you've learned?

11

Conclusion

The Invitation

We've reached the end of this book, but not the end of the journey. In fact, if you've understood what I've been saying, you know the journey never ends this side of heaven. There is no arrival point and no graduation from the wobble or from the discipleship journey, no moment when you can say, "I've figured this out. I'm done navigating now." There's only the ongoing, daily, moment-by-moment work of following Jesus through whatever conditions you find yourself in.

So this isn't really a conclusion. It's an invitation.

- An invitation to stop living the lie of the straight line path in discipleship and embrace the reality of the wobble.
- An invitation to stop performing discipleship and start practicing it.
- An invitation to take responsibility for your actions and attitudes and stop making excuses.
- An invitation to navigate faithfully rather than drift passively.

What This Isn't

- This isn't an invitation to adopt my system, especially since I don't have a system. I have principles I've learned through decades of wobbling, and tools that have helped me navigate. But your journey is yours alone. The Holy Spirit is creating a path for you that no one else has walked.
- This isn't an invitation to mimic my life. I've shared my stories not as a template, but as examples - some good, many not so good. Your circumstances are different. Your patterns are different. Your wobble will look different than mine.
- This isn't an invitation to lower your standards. Embracing the wobble doesn't mean accepting mediocrity or rationalizing disobedience. It means pursuing Christ-likeness with honest assessment of where you actually are, not where you pretend to be.
- This isn't an invitation to comfortable faith. What I'm describing is harder than the straight-line myth. It requires more honesty, more responsibility, more engagement, more persistence.
- This isn't an invitation to perfect anything. You won't perfect the wobble. You won't perfect your navigation. You won't perfect your discipleship. You'll just keep showing up, keep adjusting, keep following faithfully, imperfectly, for the rest of your life.

What This Is

- This is an invitation to authenticity. To stop maintaining the gap between who you present yourself to be and who you actually are. To bring your Monday reality to Sunday morning. To be the same person in every aspect of your life.
- This is an invitation to responsibility. To own your actions and attitudes completely. To stop blaming circumstances, others, your past, or even "how God made you" for choices that you make.
- This is an invitation to embrace the process over arrival. To value the journey of formation over the fantasy of perfection. To embrace becoming

rather than pretending you've already become.
- This is an invitation to community. To stop trying to navigate alone. To give people actual access to your life. To speak truth and receive truth in mutual relationship with fellow wobblers.
- This is an invitation to honesty about the tensions. To stop collapsing conviction or certainty or zeal into one pole because you can't tolerate ambiguity. To hold the fullness of following Christ even when it's complex and uncomfortable.
- This is an invitation to the long view. To measure your growth over years and decades, not days and weeks. To trust the Holy Spirit's work even when you can't see it in the moment. To press on faithfully whether you feel like you're making progress or not.

Most fundamentally, this is an invitation to follow Jesus as He actually is, not as we've imagined Him to be.

- Not the Jesus who demands perfection, but the Jesus who says "follow Me" to imperfect people and patiently leads them through their wobbling.
- Not the Jesus of the straight line, but the Jesus who meets Peter in his denial, Thomas in his doubt, and the disciples in their fear and still calls them His own.
- Not the Jesus who requires arrival before relationship, but the Jesus who enters into relationship right where you are and then begins the lifelong work of formation.

This is the Jesus I've been following for decades. This is the Jesus I'm still learning to follow. This is the Jesus who is faithful when I'm not, patient when I'm impatient with myself, and persistent in His work of making me more like Him.

CONCLUSION

Where Do You Start?

Maybe you're reading this and thinking, "Okay, I see it. I see the wobble. I see the performance trap I've been in. I see the straight-line myth I've been believing. But where do I actually start?" Start with honesty. Stop right now and do an honest assessment:

- Where am I actually in my discipleship? Not where I wish I was. Not where I should be. Not where I was last year. Where am I right now?
- What's the gap between my public persona and my private reality? Where am I performing instead of being authentic?
- What am I blaming on circumstances or other people that I'm actually responsible for?
- Where am I drifting instead of navigating?

Write it down. Be specific. Be brutally honest. You can't navigate from a position you can't pinpoint. Then take one step. Not ten steps. Not a complete overhaul. One step at a time.

- Maybe it's reaching out to one person and asking if they'd be willing to meet regularly for honest conversation about your discipleship journey.
- Maybe it's establishing one consistent practice such as 15 minutes of Scripture reading each day, a weekly self-assessment, a monthly time of extended prayer.
- Maybe it's setting one boundary that will protect you from a pattern you keep falling into.
- Maybe it's having one difficult conversation you've been avoiding.
- Maybe it's confessing one specific struggle to one trusted person instead of maintaining the pretense that you have it all together.
- Maybe it's asking God one specific question about one specific area where you're wobbling and then actually listening for His answer.

Take one step from your current position in the direction of Christ. Then take the next step. And the next and the next. That's how navigation works. Not dramatic overhauls, not New Year's resolution energy that only lasts three weeks. Just consistent, faithful, small adjustments over time.

A Word About Failure

You're going to fail. You're going to drift. You're going to make mistakes. You're going to fall back into old patterns. You're going to disappoint yourself. You're going to wobble wildly sometimes. You're going to forget everything in this book and revert to performance or passivity or blame. That's not if. That's when. And when it happens, here's what you do:

Acknowledge it honestly. Don't minimize it. Don't rationalize it. Don't explain it away. "I drifted. I made a mistake. I failed to take responsibility."

Repent where needed. If you sinned, confess it. If you hurt someone, make it right. If you broke a commitment, own it. Repentance isn't just feeling bad, it's actually changing direction.

Learn what you can. What happened? What led to the drift? What pattern are you seeing? What do you need to do differently next time?

Get back to navigating. Don't wallow. Don't spiral into self-condemnation. Don't use the failure as evidence that you should give up. Course-correct and keep moving forward. Press on.

This is the rhythm of discipleship. Navigate, drift, course-correct, navigate. Over and over and over. The goal isn't to eliminate the drift. The goal is to recognize it sooner and recover faster. Failure isn't the end of the journey. Failure is part of the journey. It's how you learn. It's how you grow. It's how you develop the sensitivity to recognize when you're off course.

> The only real failure is giving up. Or pretending you're not failing when you are, which is just another form of giving up.
>
> *So fail. Learn. Adjust. Keep going.*

CONCLUSION

The Wobble Factor - A Life Principle

The wobble factor isn't just a concept for this book. It's a principle for your entire life as a disciple.

- It's how you'll understand your marriage when you and your spouse are navigating tensions and differences.
- It's how you'll parent when your kids are learning and making mistakes and finding their own way.
- It's how you'll approach your work when you're balancing competing priorities and values.
- It's how you'll handle suffering when life circumstances don't match your expectations or prayers.
- It's how you'll engage culture when you're trying to be in the world but not of it.
- It's how you'll navigate every relationship, every decision, every season with the understanding that you're not trying to achieve a perfect straight line. You're trying to faithfully follow Christ through whatever conditions you encounter.
- The wobble factor gives you a framework for all of life. It helps you see that the course corrections, the tensions, the mistakes and recoveries. These aren't aberrations. They're normal and they're expected. They're how growth actually happens.

Over time, as you consistently apply the principles in this book and accept the principles of responsibility, authenticity, process over arrival, preparation over prediction, consistency over intensity, community over independence the amplitude decreases. The corrections become smaller. The recovery becomes faster and the navigation becomes more skilled.

> Not perfect. Never perfect. But measurably better over years and decades.
> *That's what I want for you. Not perfection. Not arrival. Just faithful,*

honest, engaged navigation through your unique journey with Christ.

A Challenge

Let me challenge you with the same question I've challenged myself with for years. Do you want to be a casual Christian or a true disciple? A casual Christian attends church when convenient, prays when in crisis, reads the Bible occasionally, gives when it doesn't cost much, serves when it fits the schedule, and maintains a generally moral life. They're sincere. They believe in Jesus. But they're not actually following Him, they're just including Him in a life they're already living.

A true disciple orients his or her entire life around following Christ. You take responsibility for your own growth, engage with Scripture and prayer consistently, you engage in authentic community, you hold tensions without collapsing them and you navigate faithfully through whatever conditions they encounter. You wobble all the time but you wobble toward Christ, not away from Him.

The difference isn't perfection. It's not about doing everything right. It's about whether you're actually engaged in the journey or just maintaining religious habits. It's about whether you take full responsibility for your discipleship or blame your lack of growth on your schedule, your stage of life, your church, your past, or anything else other than yourself.

It's about whether you're willing to be honest about where you actually are or you're committed to maintaining the performance. It's about whether you'll embrace the wobble as how discipleship actually works or you'll keep judging yourself by the myth of the straight line.

> *How you live out your discipleship journey is your choice and your responsibility.*

The life of a true disciple is harder in many ways. It requires more honesty. More responsibility. More engagement. More vulnerability. More persistence. It's also incomparably richer. More authentic. More connected. More transformative. More alive. You're made for this. You're made in God's image. You're called to this journey. The Holy Spirit is ready to guide you through it.

The question is: Will you actually follow Him?

What's Next

If this book is the foundation, what's next? The books in this series will drill deeper into the specific wobble patterns and how to recognize when you're wobbling toward conviction versus compromise, how to navigate seasons of doubt without abandoning faith, how to balance zeal with wisdom in specific life decisions.

We'll explore the practical disciplines and tools in more detail and how to build sustainable rhythms, how to structure authentic community, and how to practice spiritual disciplines in ways that actually form you rather than becoming empty rituals. We'll look at specific life stages and situations where the wobble intensifies as you navigate career transitions, handle suffering and loss, raise children as a disciple, steward your resources, engage in culture.

But you don't need to wait for the next book to start navigating. Everything you need to begin is already in your hands. You understand the myth and the reality. You know the tensions you're navigating. You have the principles to guide you. You have the tools to practice. You know what authentic community looks like and why you need it. You understand how to measure growth over time.

Now you just need to do it.

The Invitation Stands

I Am Responsible and I wobble. That's the foundation. That's the starting point. That's the non-negotiable truth that everything else builds on. You are responsible for your discipleship. Not your pastor. Not your small group. Not your spouse. Not your circumstances. You.

The Wobble Factor is how you navigate that responsibility. It's the reality of how discipleship actually works. It's the pattern you'll live in for the rest of your life.

And Pilocon (Piloted Connections) describes the harbor pilot navigating through changing conditions toward the sure destination holds it all together. That's what you're becoming. Not a passenger, not someone on autopilot, but an active, engaged navigator following the Holy Spirit's leading through the waters you find yourself in.

The invitation stands. It will always stand. Because God is always calling disciples to follow, always working to form them, always patient with their wobbling, always faithful in His formation.

- Will you accept the invitation?
- Will you stop performing and start practicing?
- Will you take responsibility and start navigating?
- Will you embrace the wobble as the reality of faithful discipleship?

The journey awaits. The Spirit is ready to lead. The community is here to support you. All that's needed is for you to take the first honest, responsible, faithful step. So take it, then take the next one, and the next.

All the way home. This is just the beginning.

The Wobble Factor: Reclaiming the Truth of the Journey

About the Author

<u>My Prayer for You</u>

I first penned the following prayer over three decades ago, but it is still relevant in my life today. Seeing how God continually works in our lives as we move through this journey on earth with Him is amazing. We have no idea what He has in store for us, which is exciting and daunting at the same time. Little did I know how long-lasting the words of this poem that became a prayer would be and how it would still describe my feelings all these years later – but God did.

Lord Make Me a Marathon Man
   by Ron Robison
   I give my body and spirit to you
   Mold and shape me to your image
   Train my body to run your race for victory
   Feed my mind with knowledge of your world
   Help my eyes to focus on you
   Give me a heartbeat with a passion for your work

Increase my lung capacity to breathe in all your wonders
Strengthen my arms to hold others close in times of trouble
Guide my hands to grasp your purpose in my life
Move my feet to carry the gospel to the unchurched
Train my spirit to realize all you have for me
I need a sprinter's spirit
Giving all I have to you
Running as fast as I can
To reach and stretch toward the finish line
I need a marathoner's mentality
A discipline to train for the long race
Knowing there will be ups and downs
And to look to you first to recover from injuries
Thank you for your blessings and faithfulness in me
I can do all things through you who strengthens me

You can connect with me on:
🌐 https://pilocon.com

Subscribe to my newsletter:
✉ https://www.curiouspondering.com

www.ingramcontent.com/pod-product-compliance
Lightning Source LLC
Chambersburg PA
CBHW070455090426
42735CB00012B/2558